Making the Grace Connection:

LIVING UNDER GRACE

VOL. 1: BASIC GRACE

David Ashwell

MAKING THE GRACE CONNECTION: Living Under Grace
Volume I: BASIC GRACE
Copyright © 2011 by David F. L. Ashwell

ISBN: 1469908042
ISBN-13: 9781469908045

Printed in the United States of America

This book is dedicated
To the eternal glory of God,
To those too numerous to mention by name, who have
taught me, challenged me, encouraged me and blessed me,
To all the congregation of Grace Bible Fellowship
And especially to
Jonathan and Drew
and to my beloved wife
Judith Ann Ashwell (1946-2011)
At rest in God's glorious grace.

TABLE OF CONTENTS

INTRODUCTION

Studying the Bible is not the easiest thing you will ever do, but it is without a doubt the most important thing you will ever do. It is also a deeply rewarding task if you plan on living according to what the Bible teaches and I am assuming this is why you want to *Make the Grace Connection*.

Others, besides you and me, have found the study of the Scriptures to be difficult at times. In Acts, chapter eight, we read that God sent Stephen to help the Ethiopian eunuch grasp what he was reading from Isaiah. In II Peter 3:16 the Apostle referred to the writings of the Apostle Paul "as also in all his letters, speaking in them of these things, in which are some things hard to understand, which the untaught and unstable distort, as they do also the rest of the Scriptures, to their own destruction." Be reminded Satan is always looking for someone to devour.

Speaking of destruction, you will encounter the destruction of certain 'sacred cows' we are all familiar with. When this happens to you, do not hastily dismiss what you are reading without first praying and consulting God's Word! After all, I am not untaught nor am I particularly unstable, and my fervent prayer has long been that I never distort a word of God's truth. I hope we will always be guided by "*thus sayeth the Lord*."

Devotion to the truth of Scripture is imperative. There is nothing worse than being unsure about our standing before God [is He happy or angry with me?], suffering from guilt over our frequent failures, or just being Biblically ignorant. If the word of God is correctly understood and applied, it will build our confidence in Christ and encourage us to a life of powerful faith and useful service. Grace, as you will soon discover, is full of wonderful surprises you do not want to miss. May God bless your study of this book as an aid in realizing God's sovereign grace in your life!

Chapter One
THE GIFT

WHAT IS GRACE AND WHAT DOES IT ACTUALLY DO?

Over the past forty years of studying and teaching the Bible, I have arrived at this conclusion: The one absolutely crucial and indispensable *truth* of the Bible is the eternal and supernatural *grace* of God. I have not arrived at this conclusion easily or carelessly.

Grace is the expression of God's righteous character, His glorious nature, His unending love, and His predetermined will. *Grace* is the only reason for the creation of humanity, our fall into sin, and our redemption from that fall. Only *grace* explains why Jesus would leave heaven and come to earth to reveal God to us and to rescue us by dying on a cross.

By *grace*, Jesus was born in a manger and actually lived among us for some thirty-three years. By *grace*, Jesus was executed by public crucifixion, was buried in another man's tomb, raised from the dead, and ascended into heaven. All of this was done according to the *grace* and *preordained plan* of God to save us.

Grace is the *only* basis for our salvation, and therefore, it is only *grace* that provides us the way to God and to Heaven. Grace isn't just a stepping stone into spiritual life; it is the solid foundation and only source of spiritual life. For this reason, the *grace of God* is the most important topic you and I could ever devote ourselves to studying.

When we say *God loves you*, we are talking about God's *grace*, not about God feeling sorry for us or about God trying to find something good in us that is worth loving. Therefore it is crucial that every Christian discover and make this incredible *grace connection*.

1

Since this book is about understanding God's grace, this is probably a good time to give an overview of what grace accomplishes for and in us. This overview of God's grace and the various works His grace accomplishes is presented in the form of an acrostic along with some relevant Scriptures concerning each of these facts or functions of God's *grace*.

> **G.........GRACE IS A _GIFT_ FROM GOD!** Grace cannot be earned or deserved by our conduct or good works, and neither can we be the cause for it to be **withdrawn**! GRACE describes the character, motives, and works of God. Romans 5:15; Ephesians 2:8-9
>
> **R.........GRACE HAS _REDEEMED_ US!** To be REDEEMED is to be purchased or bought back. By GRACE, Christ has redeemed us from the devil. The price for our redemption was His blood.   Galatians 3:13
>
> **GRACE HAS _REGENERATED_ US!** To be REGENERATED means to be reborn or born again. Titus 3:5, John 3:3-16
>
> **GRACE IS _RENEWING_ US**! Being renewed is learning to think andact spiritually as God does [note that it is a *process!!*]. Romans 12:2
>
> **A.........GRACE _ACQUITS_ US!** According to Romans 6:23, the penalty for sin is DEATH. Christ paid the penalty for all believers' sins. Our debt has been paid in full for all time. We are acquitted of our sin and guilt, never to be tried again.   Romans 5:18; 8:31-34
>
> **C..........GRACE _CONFORMS_ US**! It is God's specific will that we are to be changed until we are the very image of our Savior, a process that extends one moment past the end of our life on earth. Romans 8:28-30
>
> **E...........GRACE _ENABLES_ US!** God's will never sends us where His GRACE will not keep us. God's GRACE prepares, equips, and enables us to do His will and to endure. Eph. 2:10; Phil. 2:13; Heb. 13:20-21

Most of us have been taught that grace means God's free gift of salvation through Christ. While this is absolutely true, this definition is also a dangerous over-simplification of grace. Just as God's Laws formed the heart of the Old Covenant or Testament, so does God's grace form the heart of the New Covenant or Testament. No born again Christian is under the Law; we are all under God's grace *forever*.

Over simplifying God's grace makes it more difficult to grasp because grace is describing a brand new and entirely different relationship between God, Jesus, and our selves. Prior to the appearance of Jesus Christ, we were all under the Law. Obedience to the Law should bring us closer to God. This is not a difficult concept to grasp but it is *impossible* for us to do.

The Law requires each one to keep *all* of the Laws *all* of the time. Under the Law, our acceptance by God is based on our performance in keeping or obeying the Law. Unfortunately our performance is always falling short because our performance is always less than perfect.

On the other hand, grace is God's way of doing everything He wants done while providing us with everything we need, beginning with His forgiveness and *unconditional acceptance*. What God initially wants and what we unquestionably need is to be free from the shackles of sin and evil so we can live freely with God throughout eternity. Laws can't achieve this; only God's grace can.

THE DIFFERENCE BETWEEN GRACE AND RELIGION

Religion is defined as "people's beliefs and opinions concerning the existence, nature, and worship of a deity or deities." It can also refer to "an institutionalized or personal system of beliefs and practices relating to the divine," and even to any "set of strongly-held beliefs, values, and attitudes that somebody lives by." [1]

The obvious problem with religion is that it is based on "*people's beliefs and opinions*" and not necessarily on God's revealed Word in Scripture. Moreover, this failure is not merely one of the problems associated with 'fringe' religious groups and cults. No, this is becoming a widespread problem in mainline denominations and even in the evangelical establishment. There are no shortages of religions in our world. From Buddhism, Christianity, Hinduism, Islam, and Judaism to Mormonism, Scientology, Voodoo, Wiccans, and Animism, there are plenty of religions to go around. This plethora of religions gives an individual many options to pick and choose from. If a person doesn't agree with what one group says, they can usually find another group that does agree with them.

Although the teachings of various religions may differ considerably from one group to another, there are also some cunning *similarities* between them, which we need to carefully watch for. Anyone who is seeking spiritual guidance must know how to recognize these *similarities* and be careful to harvest only Biblically revealed truth.

For example, one thing all religions have in common is a *set of rules or laws* governing the beliefs, worship, and conduct of their followers. Of course, many of these laws and rules bare a striking similarity to the Bible. For example, most religions forbid and condemn murder, theft, rape, adultery, and fornication. Some groups are more lenient about morality than others, but still insist on some standards, even if it is only to not judge others. Consequently many religions also typically teach on human relationships and on having a social conscience.

Christianity is no different in this respect. We share the same Ten Commandments or Laws with Judaism. Christians are told to love their fellow brothers and sisters, to not be judgmental, and to help others in times of need. These commonalities have prompted many to believe that paying too much attention to any one religion, to the exclusion of all the others, only promotes religious intolerance and is totally counterproductive. After all, since all 'religions' have so much in common, they are all like spokes of the same wheel, and lead to the same 'hub' or god. In this kind of environment, truth becomes subjective and loses its authority and relevance.

GOD'S GRACE IS UNIQUE

There is one religion that is uniquely different from all other religions, despite certain similarities, and it is Christianity. In fact, many Christians do not like to refer to Christianity as a religion because of this uniqueness. The exceptional difference in Christianity is that it worships the loving God of *grace*, not a god of harsh and unforgiving rules.

From time to time various religions use words like grace, but their concept of grace does not define the true and complete meaning of Biblical grace. The grace of God revealed in the Holy Bible is very specific and vastly more important then many Christians realize, for grace *is* true Christianity!

The Biblical Greek word for grace is *charis* and refers to a gift which is freely given or bestowed on someone in the form of a favor, care or help and goodwill. For Christian believers, grace means the undeserved gift of eternal salvation, the gift of the indwelling Holy Spirit, and the different and unique spiritual abilities or gifts to enable a Christian to function effectively in their service to God.

Grace is the free gift of salvation from God through the crucifixion of Jesus Christ as just payment for the consequences of sin in a person's life. No other religions have a Savior nor admit to the necessity of a Savior to save humans from their sins. Salvation from sin by our Savior the Lord Jesus Christ *is* grace, and it is the totally unique difference of Christianity.

Religions approach the problem of human frailty and error [they hate that word *sin*] with the assumption that rules or laws are what we humans need to get our lives straightened out. On the other hand, although Christianity also has rules or Laws, such as the Ten Commandments, these Laws were given by God to mankind for a distinctly different purpose.

For us, the Law exists to convince us of our total *inability* to keep or obey God's Laws despite our own strength and resolve. Christianity has no Laws designed to grant salvation if they are kept, because the point is that no one, except Jesus the Son of God, can keep all of them. Instead, the Laws in Christianity exist to convict us and to convince us of our absolute need for salvation through Christ Jesus. It is written in Galatians 3:21-25, "Is the Law then contrary to the promises of God? May it never be! For if a law had been given which was able to impart life, then righteousness would indeed have been based on law. But the Scripture has shut up everyone under sin, so that the promise by faith in Jesus Christ might be given to those who believe. But before faith came, we were kept in custody under the law, being shut up to the faith which was later to be revealed. Therefore the Law has become our tutor to lead us to Christ, so that we may be justified by faith. But now that faith has come, we are no longer under a *tutor* [i.e. the Law]."

OUR NEED FOR GOD'S AUTHENTIC GRACE

Many well-intentioned Christians still believe that the essential core of Christianity is God's commandments and Laws. Although most of these well-intentioned "stumbling blocks" agree that we are saved by faith or grace, when it comes to living the Christian life on a daily basis, they fall back and rely on laws, rules, and guilt to motivate them in the direction they believe a Christian must take. For most Christians even though they do not realize it, when it comes to daily living, their 'Christianity' reverts back to being just another religion with rules and laws to be obeyed, or else!

Fortunately for every Christian, we have a unique birthright guaranteed to us by God. Our birthright is life in the freedom and power of God's grace as it is ministered to us daily by the indwelling Spirit of Jesus Christ. The grace of God is intended to enable *every* Christian *every* step of the way until we stand fully glorified in God's presence with His full and complete approval.

Invariably, whenever Christians discuss grace, the caveat that "… nevertheless, we are still responsible" always seems to be the final conclusion. It is as if to say, "Grace is all well and good, but man is still responsible to obey the Laws of God," never mind that man is incapable of obeying or keeping the Law as it is required. It grieves me greatly to see Christians and the message of grace repeatedly *thrown under the bus*. We are mistakenly told that no matter what we say, in our hearts we still believe that we must perform correctly to receive God's acceptance.

You and I do have a responsibility to learn Biblical truth and learn to apply it correctly by faith. But even this requires the work of God through the Holy Spirit within us. Jesus said to His followers in John 16:7-14, "But I tell you the truth, it is to your advantage that I go away; for if I do not go away, the Helper will not come to you; but if I go, I will send Him to you. And He, when He comes, will convict the world concerning sin and righteousness and judgment; concerning sin, because they do not believe in Me; and concerning righteousness, because I go to the

Father and you no longer see Me; and concerning judgment, because the ruler of this world has been judged. I have many more things to say to you, but you cannot bear them now. But when He, the Spirit of truth, comes, He will guide you into all the truth; for He will not speak on His own initiative, but whatever He hears, He will speak; and He will disclose to you what is to come. He will glorify Me, for He will take of Mine and will disclose it to you."

The Apostle Paul clearly exhorts us in Romans 12:2, saying, "And do not be <u>conformed</u> to this world, but be <u>transformed</u> by the renewing of your mind." The renewing of our minds occurs as we study and apply the truths of the Bible by faith through the enablement and guidance of the Spirit. Always remember John 14:26, which says "But the Helper, the Holy Spirit, whom the Father will send in my name, He will teach you all things, and bring to your remembrance all that I said to you." Biblical Christianity cannot be *discovered* or *lived* apart from the work of the Spirit.

GOD'S WORD AND GRACE

Many religions have 'holy' books. However, the authorship of these books is often questionable, as are many of the assertions these books make. L. Ron Hubbard, a successful fiction writer, claimed that anyone could start a religion, and then proved it by writing his book on *Scientology*. The Mormons have the *book of Mormon*, the Muslims have the *Koran,* and the Christian Scientists have *Science and Health with Key to the Scriptures* by Mary Baker Eddy. The Jews have the Old Testament portion of the Bible but also rely heavily on a commentary on the Law called the *Torah*.

Christians also get caught up with literature outside of the Bible. Hal Lindsey's *The Late Great Planet Earth* or Dr. Tim LaHaye's *Spirit Controlled Temperament* are good examples. Rick Warren's *The Purpose Driven Life* is another, more recent example. These books can be extremely popular and even helpful, but what they teach still needs to pass the test of Scripture. All Christian literature, no matter how popular or classic, must pass this test: *Is it Biblically correct?* And without question, *this* book must pass this test as well, especially since it is intended to be a guide and commentary on the grace of God as revealed in the Scriptures!

The Apostle John tells us in I John 4:1, "Beloved, do not believe every spirit, but test the spirits to see whether they are from God; because many false prophets have gone out into the world." This verse makes it abundantly clear that anything we write or read and rely on must clearly present the Lord Jesus Christ as the only unique Son of God and our sole Savior. We always need to ask God if the assertions and comments we make are Biblically true *and* accurate.

TRUSTING GOD'S WORD

Anyone who seeks to understand the Christian faith, or wants to discuss it or even challenge it, will have to agree to do so using the Bible as the objective authority. Throwing religious or philosophical opinions back and forth will change nothing and help no one. Moreover, anyone who seeks to understand the Christian faith must agree to approach the Bible with an open mind and heart, realizing that the Bible itself claims to be nothing less than the inspired Word of God. Any attempt to teach or discuss the Christian faith must begin with this presupposition about the Bible otherwise our efforts will be in vain. Biblical ignorance can not be remedied by 'people pooling their ignorance.'

Aside from the Ten Commandments which were carved into two stone tablets by God personally, our Bible comes to us through human writers who were *led* or *inspired* to write down exactly what God wanted said. The writing of the 66 books of the Bible occurred over a period of approximately 1,500 years and was done by over 40 writers. Yet from Genesis to Revelations there is no disagreement among believers over the theme or purpose of the Scriptures. This complete internal agreement of the Bible with itself is another significant evidence for the Bible's divine authorship.

The Bible attests to its inspiration by God in both the Old and New Testaments. King David, a prophet and the writer of most of the Book of Psalms, made this revealing statement; "The Spirit of the Lord <u>spoke</u> by me, And <u>His word</u> was on my tongue." [II Samuel 23:2] The Apostle Paul said in II Timothy 3:16, "All Scripture is inspired by God and profitable for *teaching*, for *reproof*, for *correction*, for *training in righteousness*; that the man of God may be adequate, equipped for every good work." II Peter 2:20-21 says, "But know this first of all, that no prophecy of Scripture is a matter of one's own interpretation, for no prophecy was ever made by an act of human will, but <u>men moved by the Holy Spirit spoke from God.</u>"

Satan cannot destroy the inspired Word of God either, but not for lack of effort. Since Satan cannot get rid of God's Word, he will keep on trying to *disguise, distort*, and *conceal* it. Satan has and will continue to encourage careless or misleading translations of the Bible, especially those that are made by *only one person*. No matter how sincere, careful, or intelligent *one person* is, he or she is going to inevitably introduce some of their own presuppositions and biases into their work without even realizing it. Two popular examples of single author translations of the Bible are <u>The Living Bible</u> and the <u>Amplified New Testament</u>. They are fine if used to *supplement* your study of the Bible, but they are *not reliable* as Scriptural authority.

UNDERSTANDING GOD'S WORD

The greater the lack of biblical knowledge in today's churches, the easier it is for Satan to deceive us by *misinterpreting* and/or *misapplying* God's Word. We have all heard that toxic, lethal phrase, "*the Bible can be interpreted in many different ways*," or "*the Bible is subject to each person's own interpretation*," or words to that effect. These words are music to Satan's ears!

We can and should know how to accurately handle the Word of God [II Timothy 2:15], and we can also count on the Holy Spirit to "guide us into all the truth." [John 16:13] This section is about how to *read, study*, and *understand* the Bible. There are certain principles or laws for understanding God's Word along with the Holy Spirit who is teaching us what we need to know.

There are *three* distinct phases in *understanding* a Biblical passage. The first thing we need to do is to *determine accurately what the passage **says***. Since most of us are not up on our Hebrew and Greek, we should be using the most *accurate* English translation. I know there is much confusion over which English translation is best. By best I mean the one which offers the translation that is *closest* to the original language and meaning.

Some translations focus on *accuracy* while others focus on *readability* in English. Some focus on neither. Fundamentalists in particular, swear by the Authorized or King James Version. It was translated into English in the early sixteen hundreds and reads like Shakespeare, with its Thee's, Thy's, and Thou's. It contains many archaic words and phrases which our Twenty First Century ears are not accustomed to and the fact is it is not the most accurate translation of the New Testament Greek manuscripts either.

Although the New International Version is very popular these days, I have found that the New American Standard Bible from the Lockman Foundation is the best English translation of the original Greek, and therefore I use it, highly recommend it, and quote it extensively in this book.

Once we accurately know what a passage says, the second thing we need to do is *determine accurately what the passage **means***. These first two phases are *objective* in nature, although many poorly taught Christians think it means different things to different people. This is an outrageous and dangerous notion to believe. If language has any meaning, and it does, then it can't be translated to *say* whatever the translator feels it should say. The same principle holds true for determining what a passage *means*. Some languages are more specific than others, but one of the most precise languages ever is Koine Greek, the language of the New Testament.

The *interpretation* of a Biblical passage is **not** subject to many different interpretations. If you say to your girlfriend, "I love you," this does not mean you just proposed to her, although she may want it to mean that. If she goes around telling all her friends you just proposed to her, all I can say is I'm glad I'm not in your shoes. Accuracy in communication counts!

The difficulty in accurately interpreting the Bible comes when we realize it isn't saying what we wanted to hear. For our Christian doctrines to mean anything, they must be based on what the Bible *actually* teaches. When the Pharisees and the scribes questioned Jesus about some things His disciples were doing, He rebuked them saying, "Rightly did Isaiah prophesy of you hypocrites, as it is written, 'This people honors Me with their lips, but their heart is far away from Me. But in vain do they worship Me, **teaching as doctrines the precepts of men**.' Neglecting the commandment of God, you hold to the tradition of men." [Mark 7:6-8]

There are a multitude of resources on Koine Greek to aid us in determining the precise meaning of a Greek word or phrase. Many of these resources are set up for English readers to use. Nevertheless, we still have to let the Scriptures teach us, not the other way around. Open minds are important, but open hearts and a teachable spirit are even more important! Pray for a teachable heart and mind whenever you study the Word.

Once we have accurately determined what a particular passage actually *says* and *means*, we come to the third phase which is to *accurately determine how this passage applies **to my life***. However, since we are all different from each other in many ways, the *application* of a truth will vary. Who I am, how I was raised, what I do for a living, where I live, how old I was when I came to Christ and my current level of spiritual maturity all make a difference on how this passage may apply to my life. "Do not think more highly of yourself than you ought to think" [Rom. 12:3] might apply quite differently to a Bible professor having just acquired tenure, to a multi-millionaire who is thinking about starting a charitable foundation, and to someone with a family to support who just got laid off. What does it **say**; what does it **mean**; how does it **apply to me**?

UNDERSTANDING THE PRIORITIES IN GOD'S WORD

Hermeneutics, from the Greek word *hermeneia* meaning translation or interpretation, examines and explains the logical principles that govern how **all** literature must be interpreted. *Sacred Hermeneutics* focuses specifically on applying these principles to interpreting the Bible. Every student of the Bible needs to know about them, understand why they are important, and follow them. Sacred Hermeneutics gives us *four basic principles* for interpreting the Scriptures correctly.

1. THE NEW TESTAMENT DEFINES AND EXPLAINS THE OLD TESTAMENT.

Entire denominations violate this rule, not to mention many individual Christians. For example, in the Old Testament the fourth Commandment says to remember the Sabbath to keep it Holy. The Jewish Sabbath was *Saturday*, and still is. It was a day of rest, and a time for families to worship. No work, including cooking was allowed nor trips beyond what was called a 'Sabbath Day's journey', about 1/8 of a mile.

For example, there is no reference in the New Testament anywhere about keeping the Sabbath Day holy in any literal sense [although there is in a spiritual sense]. Yet the Seventh Day Adventists for one hold Church services on Saturdays, not Sundays, because they believe they must still keep the Sabbath. Devout Adventists won't even work on a Saturday.

Why is it important to hold the New Testament in higher regard over the Old Testament? Doesn't the Bible itself say "All Scripture is inspired by God?" [II Timothy 3:16] It is true that "All Scripture is inspired by God," but that doesn't mean God can't or hasn't used a hierarchy in His revelations to us.

There are clear differences between the Old and New Covenants which the Scriptures repeatedly indicate. One of the clearest is Hebrews 8:7-13, which quotes Jeremiah 31:31-34, and says, "For if that first covenant [meaning the Old Covenant of Laws] had been faultless, there would have been no occasion sought for a second. For finding fault with them, He says, 'Behold, days are coming, says the Lord, When I will effect a new covenant [grace] With the house of Israel and with the house of Judah; Not like the covenant which I made with their fathers On the day when I took them by the hand To lead them out of the land of Egypt; For they did not continue in My covenant, And I did not care for them, says the Lord. For this is the covenant that I will make with the house of Israel After those days, says the Lord: I will put My Laws into their minds, and I will write them upon their hearts. And I will be their God, And they shall be My people. And they shall not teach everyone his fellow-citizen, And every one his brother, saying "know the Lord," For all shall know Me, From the least to the greatest of them. For I will be merciful to their iniquities, And I will remember their sins no more.' When He said, 'A new covenant [grace],' He has made the first [Law] obsolete. But whatever is becoming obsolete and growing old is ready to disappear."

Failure to understand and apply this principle of interpretation endangers every Christian's walk. It is important to every Christian to know for certain they are always under grace, not the Law, because without knowing about this vital distinction, we are much more easily led astray by legalism, and in extreme cases, by some of the cults.

2. THE EPISTLES EXPLAIN THE GOSPELS.

This second principle is also very important to understanding the New Covenant of grace. Although the four Gospels begin what is called the New Testament portion of the Bible, they are mostly still part of the Old Covenant. The New Covenant couldn't begin until *after* Jesus Christ had been crucified, buried, and raised, which happens near the *end* of the Gospel accounts.

This difference between the covenants and how it affects us can easily be seen from the following Scriptures. Matthew 6:9-13 records the Lord's Prayer. Most of us had to memorize this, and it is very familiar to us, perhaps a little too familiar. Countless sermons have been preached to born-again Christians based on Old Covenant principles, and this portion of the Lord's Prayer is no exception. We are exhorted to forgive others [see verse 12], because if we don't, God will not forgive us.

Now you may argue that that is exactly what verse 12 of Matthew 6 says. I agree because it does say that, but let me also point out that this is an *Old Covenant prayer*. Remember, the Old Covenant is based on the principle that man had to perform correctly in order to secure God's acceptance. So if I wanted God's forgiveness, first I had to forgive everyone who had ever offended me.

We also need to remember that the majority of all four gospels are written about the period *just prior* to the establishment of the New Covenant. The life of Jesus was lived under the Old Covenant Law. The New Covenant couldn't begin until Christ had died, been buried, and then resurrected. In fact, the disciples were told to remain in Jerusalem until they were baptized with the Holy Spirit, which occurred on the Day of Pentecost, 50 days after the crucifixion.

The good news of the New Covenant is that the old principle has been changed. Now forgiveness is based on an entirely new principle. Please look at Ephesians 4:32: "And be kind to one another, tender-hearted, forgiving each other, just as God also has forgiven you." The conduct has not changed but the *basis* or *cause* for this behavior has. Now we are told to forgive *because* we have already been forgiven!

The Bible is not in disagreement with itself, because this rule of interpretation tells us that the old has been superseded by the new. Consequently, all those sermons that admonish us to be forgiving so that God can forgive us are in error because they are based on the *wrong* principle. Our behavior is no longer a barrier between us and God, even though our behavior still needs improvement. Now we are really free to go to God and seek His enablement to do what He wishes, rather than to feel ashamed and guilty until we improve by becoming more forgiving.

One of the essential differences between the two covenants concerns *cause* and *effect*. Under the old Law covenant our actions were the *cause* and God's actions were the *effect*. Under the covenant of grace, God's actions and decisions are the *cause*, and our obedience and performance is the *effect*. This makes a huge difference if we believe we are still being held accountable for conduct based on an Old Covenant principle. So now you can see there is good reason why these rules of interpretation are so important!

3. THE CONTEXT GOVERNS THE MEANING OR INTERPRETATION.

The context may be the paragraph or chapter in which a word or phrase is used, or the context can be as broad as the whole basis of grace in the New Covenant. Sometimes, the context is the entire Bible, such as the doctrine of God, the fall of man, and the doctrine of the Christ.

Isolating words or phrases from their surroundings by taking them *out of context*, permits many twists and turns in the interpretation of Scripture that are incorrect. Questionable and even false doctrines are frequently based on single verses of Scripture. Others are built on historical accounts, usually from the Book of Acts, of unusual events that occurred during the initial formation of the Church. Other doctrines are based on no Scripture at all, but just on a set of logical assumptions.

Such doctrines may make the most sense to our secularly shaped minds, even though the clear teaching of Scripture *contradicts* these doctrines so sincerely held and taught. False doctrines always pose a serious threat to the Church, and especially to the Christian who is not a good student of the Word and is therefore Biblically ignorant.

4. THE LITERAL MEANING TAKES PRECEDENCE OVER THE FIGURATIVE.

There are several places in Scripture where figurative language is used. Some of it, as in the parable of the Wheat and the Tares, is fairly easy to understand, and anyway Jesus explains it clearly and literally so we have no excuse for not understanding. Yet many of today's doctrines ignore this parable and what it teaches entirely.

However, prophecies are often revealed in figurative terms, and trying to make literal interpretations of figurative language frequently gets us into a mess as well. The only prophecies we can understand for sure, are those which are already fulfilled, or clearly explained in the Bible.

For example, Eschatology, the study of the prophetic future, has taken several different views of the end times which are predominantly described in figurative terms. This has resulted in the *historical* view, the *post-millennial* view, the *a-millennial* view, and the *pre-millennial* view. It would seem difficult to make a definitive pronouncement on exactly what is coming, yet many churches require acceptance of one of these versions in their Statement of Faith.

Another area where we encounter the use of figurative language is with what are called the Old Testament 'shadows', or 'copies'. Hebrews 8:5 is one such place where this is referred to, and says, "... who serve a <u>copy and shadow</u> of the heavenly things, just as Moses is warned by God when he was about to erect the tabernacle; for, "See," He says, "that you make all things according to the pattern which was shown you on the mountain."

By following the Divine pattern accurately, many practices and ceremonies and even the Old Testament tabernacle became symbols that foreshadowed things that would come much later. Many of the animal sacrifices in Israel, and specifically the Passover Lamb, were foreshadowing the crucifixion of Christ.

Another form of figurative language is the *type and antitype*. An easy example of this is referred to in Hebrews 5:10 where Melchizedek, an Old Testament king, we are told was also a 'TYPE" of Christ, Christ Himself being the ANTITYPE. It is like a foot and a footprint. The footprint is the 'type' and the foot is the 'antitype' of that which was foreshadowed. The important thing is to not get into debates and arguments over figurative language, nor let figurative language outweigh that which is already clearly stated in the Scriptures.

GRACE AND THE GOAL OF SPIRITUAL MATURITY

Colossians 1:25-29 clearly and succinctly identifies the method, the mission, and the message of the New Testament Church. The Apostle Paul says, "Of this church [the body of Christ] I was made a minister according to the stewardship from God bestowed on me for your benefit, that I might fully carry out the preaching of the word of God, that is, the mystery which has been hidden from the past ages and generations; but has now been manifested to His saints, to whom God willed to make known what is the riches of the glory of this mystery among the Gentiles, which is Christ in you, the hope of glory. And we proclaim Him, admonishing every man and teaching every man with all wisdom, that we may present every man **complete** [or *mature, perfect*] in Christ. And for this purpose also I labor, striving according to His power, which mightily works within me."

We are saved by grace and we are matured by grace, plain and simple. Our goal is the completion of every believer according to the will of God. To this end, our teaching must focus on three specific goals. I Timothy 1.5 identifies these three goals; "But the goal of our instruction is love from a pure heart and a good conscience and a sincere faith."

The first goal of our instruction is **LOVE FROM A PURE HEART**. Love is both a feeling and an action that is expressed towards others. We may not always *feel* loving, but we can always *act* in a genuinely loving manner.

Genuine, sincere love has to come from a pure heart. Love from a pure heart means a love with no strings attached. Usually in this world, love has an agenda. Most commonly, we love with the expectation of being loved in return. In extreme cases, this expectation of returned love takes on a sinister aspect, leading to extreme controlling behavior and spousal abuse, both mental and physical. Love may be claimed in such a case, but it is nothing like the unconditional love that flows from a pure heart.

A pure heart is something each of us knows we do not naturally possess, and we also know that genuine, sincere, unconditional love does not spring from us naturally either. But both are possible as grace gifts from God.

To begin with, being born again means not just a change of heart, but a whole new kind of heart, a pure heart that comes to us as a gift of God's grace. A pure heart results from the cleansing of salvation. Ezekiel 11:19-20 makes this prophetic promise for those of us under the New Covenant: "And I shall give them one heart, and shall put a new spirit within them. And I shall take the heart of stone out of there flesh and give them a heart of flesh, that they may walk in My statutes and keep My ordinances, and do them. Then they will be My people, and I shall be their God."

A favorite verse of mine is Hebrews 13:9; "Do not be carried away by varied and strange teachings; for it is good for the heart to be strengthened by grace." To achieve the teaching goal of love from a pure heart, we have to start teaching GRACE in depth, because only by grace can we get a pure heart to love with.

The second goal of our instruction is a **GOOD CONSCIENCE**. To acquire a good conscience, one that is not filled with guilt and remorse, one needs to be forgiven and cleansed by the shed blood of our Lord Christ Jesus. In other words, a good conscience results from being taught the truth about our justification. Hebrews 9:14 says, " . . . how much more will the blood of Christ, who through the eternal Spirit offered Himself without blemish to God, cleanse your conscience from dead works to serve the living God?" Love from a pure heart looks outward to others, while a good conscience looks inward at our selves.

The third goal of our instruction is a **SINCERE FAITH**. Faith, of course, looks up to God. Proverbs 3:1 says, "My son, do not forget My teaching, But let your <u>heart</u> keep My commandments;" Here again is a thinly veiled reference to the New Covenant where our obedience comes from a new heart, rather than external obedience, which comes from the flesh.

Proverbs 3:5-12 supplies us with four marks of a sincere faith. The *first* and most obvious mark of a sincere faith is stated in verses 5 and 6; "Trust in the Lord with all your heart, and do not lean on your own understanding. In all your ways acknowledge Him, and He will make your paths straight."

A sincere faith does not rely on our own wisdom, understanding, or strength. We can all expect to be stretched from time to time, by situations beyond our apparent ability. This is intentional on God's part, for it is the only way we will ever learn to rely just on Him.

The *second* mark of a sincere faith is found in verses 7 and 8: "Do not be wise in your own eyes; Fear the Lord and turn away from evil. It will be healing to your body, And refreshment to your bones."

To "fear the Lord" does not mean to be afraid of Him. The 'fear' of God for a believer always means respectful, reverential awe. It is recognizing with our minds and hearts that God is absolutely sovereign and always in control of everything. Only those who are under the Law and in rebellion to His rule need to be worried.

The *third* mark of a sincere faith, according to Proverbs 3:9-10, is revealed through our financial stewardship, or lack of it. In the average church today we are admonished to *tithe*, which means to give a tenth of our income to God. Tithing is part of the Old Covenant, and a devout Jew actually gave about a *third* of his income to God, a part of which was the 10% tithe. The tithe was proportional. There was also an annual temple tax which was the same for everyone, and then there were free-will offerings.

The New Testament does NOT require ten percent of our income, but it does instruct us to give *liberally*. The way our financial gifts honor God, is when we are led to give a certain amount, and then trusting God to supply, we give that amount. It should go without saying that God will supply our needs and more, and often He will do it in such a way as to make our faith in Him even stronger. But remember, giving is an act of faith, not an investment to gain greater returns.

The *fourth* mark of sincere faith involves discipline. Proverbs 3:11-12 says, "My son, do not reject the discipline of the Lord; Or loath His reproof, For whom He loves He reproves, Even as a father the son in whom he delights." If this sounds familiar, it is because it is also quoted in Hebrews 12:5-6. The point is that if you really do trust the Lord then trust Him enough to accept His discipline. After all, discipline is not only a mark of one who has a sincere faith, it is also the mark of one who belongs to God and is loved by God.

Biblical ignorance is the biggest obstacle we face in any effort to understand and experience God's GRACE. The only way to dispel Biblical ignorance is to become a serious student of God's Word. From the Word, the promised gift of the Holy Spirit will lead us into all truth, as we learn to handle the Word of God accurately. [II Tim. 2:15]

Chapter Two
"HANDLING THE WORD OF GOD"

BIBLICAL ILLITERACY

The heart and core of the *opposition* we encounter in learning to live by grace comes from a failure to know the Bible in general and the doctrines of New Covenant grace in particular! Biblical ignorance and Biblical illiteracy does not and can not produce mature, useful, or satisfied Christians. What we don't know *will* hurt us and get in the way of our spiritual growth!

Do not misunderstand! We are *not* saying Christians are stupid; we are saying that most of today's Christians are *not* well taught. Some of the fault for this rests with the leaders and teachers in the Church, but some of the fault rests with us, too. Each and every Christian needs to insure that their Biblical education is sufficiently *adequate* and sufficiently *accurate* to render them "adequate, equipped for every good work." [II Timothy 2:15, 3:17]

The exhortation in Romans 12:2 is directed at every single Christian. It says in part, "And do not be conformed to this world, but be transformed by the renewing of your mind." The word translated "*conformed*" literally means to press something into a mold. The message for us is to *not* continue being molded by this world's thinking, but rather to be transformed and molded according to God's thinking.

The Bible says the *beginning* of wisdom is reverence [fear] for the Lord. This is where everyone must begin. Psalm 14:1a says, "The fool has said in his heart, 'There is no God.'" Those who reject the existence of God are not going to want to read and study what is claimed to be the words of this non-existent god. This is why I Corinthians 1:23-25 says, "but we preach Christ crucified, to Jews a stumbling block, and to Gentiles foolishness, but to those who are the called, both Jews and Greeks, Christ the power of God and the wisdom of God. Because the foolishness of God is wiser than men, and the weakness of God is stronger than men."

Continuing in I Corinthians 2:12-14 we further learn, "Now we have received, not the spirit of the world, but the Spirit who is from God, that we might know the things freely given to us by God, which things we also speak, not in words taught by human wisdom, but in those taught by the Spirit, combining spiritual thoughts with spiritual words. But a natural man does not accept the things of the Spirit of God; for they are foolishness to him, and he cannot understand them, because they are spiritually appraised."

"Do you believe the Bible is the Word of God" is not a trick question. If we want to understand the Bible, we will have to start by *believing* in the One Who wrote it.

It goes without saying that any author worth reading for spiritual wisdom must also believe in God. You, the reader, are responsible for discerning whether what human authors write is worth reading from a spiritual standpoint. Can the spiritual authenticity of an author be difficult to determine? Of course it can; after all, we learned that Satan loves to disguise himself as an angel of 'light.'

We are told to test the spirits for spiritual authenticity because not every 'spirit' is from God. To do this will require a growing understanding of the New Covenant and serious prayer. God will certainly send the Holy Spirit to illuminate any one who asks, just as surely as He does for those He has chosen. As it says in Proverbs 9:10, "The fear of the Lord is the beginning of wisdom, and the knowledge of the Holy One is understanding." You can also read about the promised gift of the Holy Spirit and His role in our learning process in John 16:7-13.

THE SOURCE OF GOD'S WORD

The last words of King David, the Psalmist and a prophetic writer, include this excellent comment: "The Spirit of the Lord spoke by me, and His word was on my tongue." [II Samuel 23:2]

II Timothy 3:16 begins by saying, "All Scripture is inspired by God..." The word "inspired" literally means "God-breathed." II Peter 2:20-21 goes on to say, "But know this first of all, that no prophecy of Scripture is a matter of one's own interpretation, for no prophecy was ever made by an act of human will, but men moved by the Holy Spirit spoke from God."

These Scriptures are important because they tell us who the real Author of the Bible is, and they also tell us how He communicated the Bible to us. God gave us the 66 books of the Bible over a span of some 1,500 years, through approximately 42 human writers, whom God inspired to write down exactly what He wanted said. The Bible was written originally in two languages. The Old Testament is written in Hebrew and the New Testament is written in Greek.

Most churches that believe and teach the Bible have a document known as a Statement of Faith. This is done for the benefit of those considering joining a prospective church as well as educating the existing congregation. It spells out the specific Biblical beliefs that a church holds and teaches. Most Evangelical Statements of Faith *concerning* the Bible go something like this: We believe the Bible is the *inspired, infallible*, and only *authoritative* Word of God, *completely inerrant* [without mistakes] in the original manuscripts, preserved by God, and provided by Him for the illumination and education of all Mankind.

The *infallibility* of the Bible means it is incapable of erring or failing. The Bible is completely accurate, and flawless. Some add the caveat "in matters of doctrine and dogma." This stems from many disagreements with Scripture from those in the scientific community who continue to 'worship' the golden calf of evolution and its high priest Charles Robert Darwin (1809-1882). Darwin's theory of evolution became so popular that even the Church started trying to accommodate it, fearing they would otherwise be considered irrelevant.

This is sad, because modern archeology and geology have demonstrated, purely from the scientific evidence, that the 'theory' of creation is much more valid than the theory of evolution. Besides evidence from fossils, archeology continues to confirm the Bible's historical accounts again and again.

The Bible is also *authoritative*. The best proof of this is in II Timothy 3:16-17: "All Scripture is inspired by God and profitable for teaching, for reproof, for correction, for training in righteousness; that the man of God may be adequate, equipped for every good work."

Completely inerrant in the original manuscripts is a little misleading, because if you believe as I do, that the Bible is indeed the Accurate Word of God originally, then why would it not be correct to believe that He has also protected His Word as it was transmitted from generation to generation!

THE IMPORTANCE OF GOD'S WORD

Satan cannot destroy the inspired Word of God, but not from lack of trying. For example, Dr. William F. Beck wrote, "In the persecution of A. D. 303 Emperor Diocletian ordered a systematic search that swept away the Biblical manuscripts from Asia Minor and Syria. The sacred writings were shoveled into carts and hauled to the market places to be burned. The goal was to wipe out Christianity. Later the Goths, Vandals, Moslems, and Mongols did their worst [or best] to destroy the Christian faith."[2]

Since Satan cannot get rid of God's people or God's Word, he will keep on trying to disguise, distort, and conceal it. Satan has and will continue to encourage careless or misleading translations of the Bible, especially those that have been made by *only one person*. No matter how sincere, careful, or intelligent one person is, he is going to introduce his own presuppositions and biases into his work without ever realizing it. The Living Bible is an excellent example of this, as is the Amplified New Testament. They are fine if used as *commentaries* on the Bible, but they are not sufficiently reliable translations of the Bible to base doctrine on.

God's grace is not a part of our conscious secular world. Of course, God's grace is always at work in our world although usually behind the scenes, so if we are to understand grace and consciously participate in it, we must first discover the true meaning of grace from the Scriptures. This demands that each Christian become skilled in the use of the bible.

In II Timothy 2:15 we are told, "Be diligent to present yourself approved to God as a workman who does not need to be ashamed, handling accurately the word of truth." Analyzing, interpreting and translating the Bible *correctly* is not impossible nor is it optional! Handling the word of God in a slipshod fashion not only disgraces the one who is careless and inaccurate, it also dishonors God and His word. This often does serious damage to the body of Christ and it diminishes our witness before a watching world.

Considering the importance of *how competently* we approach God's truth in our study, teaching, and in our application, II Timothy 2:15 indentifies *three objectives* we must keep in mind in our handling of the word of truth.

1. The study and teaching of God's word demands **diligence**. Errors are inevitable because we *are* merely humans, but our errors should never be the result of *carelessness* or *laziness*.

2. Secondly, our study and teaching of the Bible demands a reasonable level of **competence**. We can't all be full-blooded mainline theologians, but then again, some of these 'great' theologians are so badly flawed in their concepts, that we would be far better off without them. The Holy Spirit is the only One who can reveal the truth accurately, every Christian has equal access to Him, and every Christian is responsible to test every spirit for not all are from God.

3. Thirdly, as we have said, we should always strive for **accuracy** for our own sake as well as for the sake of those we will influence.

These three objectives are not meant to put anyone on a guilt trip or to provide us with excuses for doing nothing because we aren't perfect. This is simply meant to encourage us to take this individually necessary task seriously, and to give it our best efforts in the Spirit.

THE BENEFITS IN GOD'S WORD

II Timothy 3:15-16, along with assuring us that all Scripture is *inspired* by God, shows us four techniques or ways in which God's Word rewards us. These are tactics by which we can always expect God's Spirit to operate in our lives.

1. TEACHING: A religion that is based on a set of laws or rules, with rewards for success, and punishment for failure may be impossible to do, but it is *not* hard to understand. Most of the world's major religions, including Judaism, are fairly similar in this respect. Each has a code of conduct which must be followed, such as the Ten Commandments for

Judaism. What religion in general never seems to take into account is the certain fact that no one can follow the 'code of conduct' without regular and repeated failure.

Apart from the New Testament of the Bible, there is little difficulty in understanding how religions work. They are all basically systems that recognize and are based on right and wrong. This comes as no surprise when we remember that Genesis tells us of the sin of Adam and Eve, which resulted in the human race being burdened with the knowledge of good and evil that could only point out their flaws and mistakes to them.

Religions are also based on a system of rewards and punishments for good and bad behavior. In this way, the attempt is made to keep the followers of a religion's code or laws motivated and under control. There is no huge divergence between the codes of the various religions. Murder is always a bad and punishable behavior, while charity to the less fortunate is always a good behavior deserving of reward.

Because of this similarity between the various religions of the world, many contend that which religion one follows is not important because every religion is like one of the spokes on a wheel, which all lead to the hub. The hub of the wheel, where all the spokes connect together, is god. The belief is that all religions lead to the same one god or what-ever the various religions call him. To the secular mind this makes a lot of sense. The only problem with this 'belief' is that it is totally contradicted by the Bible, which says no one comes to the Father [God] *except by Me* [Jesus Christ]. Obviously, handling the word of God accurately is crucial.

New Testament Christianity presents a set of beliefs, which are significantly different and unique compared to all the other religions. Because this is true, it also makes authentic Biblical Christianity harder to understand. The fact is authentic Biblical Christianity does not make any sense to the secular mind. I Corinthians 2:14 explains this, saying, "But a natural [secular or unspiritual] man does not accept the things of the Spirit of God; for they are foolishness to him, and he cannot under-stand them, because they are spiritually appraised [or examined]."

2. REPROOF: The Bible is also profitable for reproof. Reproof is criti-cism for doing something incorrectly. It is a rebuke, a scolding, and a reprimand. In other words, or in any words, a reproof is not something we welcome easily, even if it is for our own good. Nevertheless, the Scripture says that *reproof*, based on the truth of Scripture, is always profitable.

The Book of Proverbs is filled with wisdom on many subjects. This includes the value and importance of *reproof*. For example, "A fool rejects his father's discipline, but he who regards reproof is prudent." "Stern discipline is for him who forsakes the way; He who hates reproof will die." "He whose ear listens to the life-giving reproof will dwell among the wise. He who neglects discipline [or reproof] despises himself, but he who listens to reproof acquires understanding. The fear [or reverence] of the Lord is the instruction for wisdom, and before honor comes humility." [Proverbs 15:5, 10, 31-33]

In every one of these quotations from Proverbs 15, *reproof* is presented as being valuable, necessary, and even desirable. Hebrews 12: 4-8 also reminds us of the importance of a Father's reproof or *discipline*; "You have not yet resisted to the point of shedding blood, in your striving against sin; and you have forgotten the exhortation which is addressed to you as sons, 'My son, do not regard lightly the discipline of the Lord, nor faint when you are reproved by Him; For those whom the Lord loves He disciplines, And He scourges every son whom He receives.' It is for discipline that you endure; God deals with you as with sons; for what son is there whom his father does not discipline? But if you are without discipline, of which all have become partakers, then you are illegitimate children and not sons."

Verse 7 states that "It is for discipline that you endure." The Greek verb is a present imperative, or *command*. It means to "keep on expecting discipline," or to "keep on enduring the discipline," because *every* true believer will be reproved and disciplined. We may not look forward to discipline, but sometimes it helps to remember that reproof is *proof* that we belong to God, that He really loves us, and that we are His legitimate heirs.

3. CORRECTION: Proverbs 16:25 says, "There is a way which seems right to a man, but its end is the way of death." Often our response to *reproof* gets us into more hot water, because *how* we *correct* a problem or situation is more important then the fact that we sinned in the first place.

Although a Christian is always *in* the Spirit, we do not always *walk* in the Spirit. Sometimes we *walk* in the flesh. Believe it or not, some Christians *walk* in the flesh *frequently*.

Between *reproof* and *correction*, there is a lot of room for guilt to rear its ugly head. In Second Corinthians 7:10, we learn that when God's Spirit convicts us of sin, He knows it will cause us sorrow and pain. However, this is the *sorrow* that leads us to repentance without regret [without guilt], causing our growth towards maturity. When God corrects us, it is done with our best interests at heart; *correction* is not about punishment, but rather it is a natural, caring act of God's love and grace to protect us, free us, and mature us.

Consider the Apostle Paul's experience on the road to Damascus. At the time, Paul [his name was actually Saul; he later changed it to Paul] was not yet a believer in Christ. In fact, he was the exact opposite, being one of the Sanhedrin's chief persecutors of the followers of Christ.

Acts 9:3-6 informs us, "And it came about that as he [Saul/Paul] journeyed, he was approaching Damascus, and suddenly a light from heaven flashed around him; and he fell to the ground, and heard a voice saying to him 'Saul, Saul, why are you persecuting Me?' And he said, 'Who art Thou Lord?' And He said, "I am Jesus whom you are persecuting, but rise, and enter the city, and it shall be told you what you must do.'"

Saul was completely blinded by that light and remained blind for three days [Acts 9:8-9]. He regained some of his sight, but eyesight was always a problem for him. His letters [epistles] were dictated, although he always wrote a personal note at the end. In one of them, Galatians 6:11, Paul said, "See with what large letters I am writing to you with my own hand." In Galatians 4:15 Paul wrote, "For I bear you witness, that if possible, you would have plucked out your eyes and given them to me." These comments suggest that Paul had continuing difficulty with his eyesight.

With this visual problem in mind, read Paul's remarks about a revelation he received and one of the results it had on him. II Corinthians 12:7 says, "And because of the surpassing greatness of the revelation, for this reason, to keep me from exalting myself, there was given me a thorn in the flesh, a messenger of Satan to buffet me -- to keep me from exalting myself!"

No one is sure if the buffeting messenger from Satan was this visual problem or not, but in any event whatever it was Paul prayed to be healed of it. In II Corinthians 12:8-10 Paul continues saying, "Concerning this I entreated the Lord three times that it might depart from me. And He has said to me, 'My grace is sufficient for you, for power is perfected in weakness.' Most gladly, therefore, I will rather boast about my weaknesses, that the power of Christ may dwell in me. Therefore I am well content with weaknesses, with insults, with distresses, with persecutions, with difficulties, for Christ's sake; for when I am weak, then I am strong."

4. TRAINING IN RIGHTEOUSNESS: Finally, the inspired Scripture is profitable for *training in righteousness. Teaching,* which is spiritual feeding, is the first step in a Christian's spiritual growth but we still need to understand how to apply these great truths we are learning. Putting what we learn into practice involves both instruction and practice. This is what *training in righteousness* is about. God's Word provides the instruction, while the Holy Spirit provides the guidance and training to understand and apply [or practice] what God teaches us. It is interesting to note that between the 'theory' and the 'practice' comes the *reproof* and *correction.* Something I have never understood is how so many Christian people who claim to believe the Bible can't seem to make any allowances, either for them selves or for others, to struggle and fail in this growth process that is absolutely necessary if we are ever to get from the doctrine [truth] to the applications [practice].

This might help to explain how the Word aids us in the training trials every one of us has to face. James 1:2-4 gives us this unusual instruction; "Consider it all joy, my brethren, when you encounter various trials [or temptations]; knowing that the testing of your faith produces endurance. And let endurance have its perfect result, that you may be perfect [mature] and complete, lacking in nothing."

Romans 5:3-5 which introduces us to the process of sanctification, also says, "And not only this, but we also exult in our tribulations; knowing that tribulation brings about perseverance; and perseverance, proven character; and proven character, hope; and hope does not disappoint; because the love of God has been poured out within our hearts through the Holy Spirit who was given to us."

Most people do *not* find trials, temptations, and tribulations something to rejoice and be happy about or to look forward to. Nevertheless, we are told to exult and consider it all joy when we hit the rough patches in life. Why? For one thing, spiritual growth does not take place in a vacuum or a test tube. Our spiritual growth occurs in real life and in real time. It is gradual, it is difficult, it is frustrating, it is painful, it can be frightening, at times it gets us dirty, and at times it leaves us feeling completely defeated and at the end of our 'rope.'

So what is there to rejoice and exult over? First of all, trials, tribulations, and discipline are *proof* that we have been saved and belong to God. It is also the only way we can be trained to be righteous. Hebrews 12:11 echoes this same sentiment: "All discipline for the moment seems not to be joyful, but sorrowful; yet to those who have been trained by it, afterwards it yields the peaceful fruit of righteousness."

God is the One in charge of our sanctification [spiritual growth], which can only be by grace through faith! We absolutely have to trust that God *always* knows what He is doing, and that He *always* knows what is best. So even though we already know this, it never hurts to have it repeated again and again! Being led is hard for humans to accept.

THE PRIORITIES OF REVELATION

Another way in which Christians manage to get themselves into a lot of trouble with the Bible, is when they start clinging to the belief that either they themselves have had a direct revelation from God, or become committed to following some charismatic personality making that claim. It is very easy to get carried away by such an experience because in our minds it presupposes that we are 'more' worthy and this gives us greater significance.

We must recognize that there are inherent and significant dangers associated with believing and obeying the content of direct revelations from God. First of all, because we are always subject to being mislead by our desires, drives and feelings, as is anyone else claiming to have a direct revelation themselves. Secondly, we are always subject to being misled by false prophets and deceitful workers Satan sends to us as 'angels of light'.

It is for this very reason that I John 4:1 warns us, "Beloved, do not believe every spirit, but test the spirits to see whether they are from God; because many false prophets have gone out into the world." The challenge for every believer is learning how to test the spirits to see if they are from God. As a very new Christian, I had a personal experience with God that may help to illustrate the three basic tests to see if a spirit is indeed from God.

I was house sitting and filling in for our Church custodian, a retired missionary, while he and his wife took a much deserved vacation. I was all alone in their house and I had drifted off into a sound sleep, when I suddenly heard a male voice speaking. It was a brief statement, which I could not make out clearly because of how soundly I sleep. This 'voice' left me in a state somewhere between awake and sound asleep. Then I heard the same voice speaking to me a second time. I was still more concerned with the fact that I was hearing a voice speaking to me in an empty house late at night than in what the voice was saying.

Although I was still laying there under the covers, I was now wide awake. And that is when I heard the voice speak a third time. The 'voice' said the same identical thing all three times, but hearing a voice speaking to you when you are wide awake in an empty house is a jarring, attention grabbing moment.

All three times he only said "II Corinthians 3:4." Although it was spoken calmly and matter-of-factly, hearing it again while wide awake propelled me straight up out of the bed. I turned on a light and grabbed for my Bible. As I was looking up this passage, I was just sure I was about to receive some great earth-shaking apocalyptic revelation from God.

My 'apocalyptic revelation' in II Corinthians 3:4 said "And such confidence we have through Christ toward God." That was it. I must honestly say that to a very new Christian, this one verse most definitely did not seem to be an apocalyptic revelation. At least this is what I thought at the time. In fact, I must admit that after the initial surprise wore off, I was actually disappointed. After all, if God had gone to this much trouble to communicate with me, how come I couldn't see any particular significance to this passage? I also wondered exactly whose voice it was that I heard, but since he never identified himself, any speculation is futile.

It has been forty years since that unusual night, and I have never had another experience like it. I have had other experiences that strongly reminded me of II Corinthians 3:4. After walking away from two fairly severe traffic accidents, surviving two heart attacks, and walking around with a burst appendix for over four months (it is extremely rare but obviously possible), I am starting to get a little more insight into just how II Corinthians 3:4 applies to me, and why I needed it. As it turns out, this verse also ended up explaining to me, to some extent, how God was planning to use me in the lives of others. I am still learning what this one verse from God means for me and to me!

Just as I was editing this book for publication I had another experience to which this verse applied. My wife of forty years got to go home to Jesus. Being granted growing confidence in God through Christ is an incredible comfort to me [but I am still jealous].

I am relating my personal experience with the Lord only because many others have also had or claim to have had unusual divine encounters. This direct revelation emphasized a verse that had an *application* that was meant only for me and my immediate family. Of course, the statement made in II Corinthians 3:4 is for every Christian, for every one of us needs confidence in Christ towards God, but the specific application to my life will probably not be the same as the application is to your life.

Many other Christians have had unusual encounters with God. For me it was purely personal and this is the first time I have ever felt led to share it publically. These kinds of experiences do not happen to us because we are some kind of super-Christian. I pray no one will read into this testimony anything that would suggest that having such an encounter sets one apart from or above others. It doesn't. On the contrary, it is my opinion that the weaker a believer is, the more they are likely to need to be propped up by some unique personal experience like this.

I would like to propose that God has given us *three* reliable witnesses to help us test the spirits to see whether they are from God or not.

They are listed here in a descending order of importance, beginning with the most important witness, the Bible.

1. THE WITNESS OF THE SCRIPTURE: This is the number one highest priority witness. It is the most important 'witness.' We must always ask, "Does what we heard or read agree with the words of Scripture and the *context* where it was found?" The Bible itself is the best and most important commentary we can get on the Bible. Almost all theological error is a result of some thought or command having first been taken out of *context* or out of agreement with the Word.

2. THE WITNESS OF THE CHURCH: This is the number two priority and could be called the historical priority. Most passages of Scripture have been understood in pretty much the same way for 2,000 years or more. This witness tells us how other Christians down through the centuries have understood a passage. For example, any passage which declares that Jesus is the Son of God is believed to be correct and not open to dispute, because in this case, both the context and the church are in complete agreement and have been since the First Century.

When Christians have historically come down on both sides of a doctrine, then the witness of the Church is of little value. In areas of doctrinal dispute, only the Bible can define what is really true, because only the Bible is completely true and always right. Only by one's own study of the Bible can anyone dispel Biblical ignorance. In the end, each one must be persuaded in their own conscience. In Philippians 3:15 the Apostle admonishes us, "Let us therefore, as many as are perfect [i.e., mature], have this attitude; and if in anything you have a different attitude, God will reveal that also to you; . . ."

3. THE WITNESS OF THE SPIRIT: This is also referred to as our *inner light*. Romans 8:16 says, "The Spirit Himself bears witness with our spirit that we are children of God." And Romans 8:14 says; "For all who are being led by the Spirit of God, these are sons of God." These are just two examples of the work of the Holy Spirit in our lives. But does the 'inner light' verify the truth or falsity of a particular doctrine? I would answer that very often the Spirit will either confirm or deny some fact within us, so that we either have peace about it, or we won't. But sometimes we will be drawn aside by other persuasive 'voices' within us.

Proverbs 12:15a warns us that "The way of a fool is right in his own eyes." Proverbs 14:12 also warns us, saying "There is a way which seems right to a man, but its end is the way of death."

Just because I decide to do something doesn't mean it is right or good. We must remember that opinions are like feet; almost everybody has them but that doesn't mean they are all walking in the right direction. I may believe God has shown me some important truth, but if He has, then it will agree, not disagree with the word of God. As in my own experience, all I received was a reference to a specific verse of Scripture. Even if I didn't really understand it at the time, the one thing I was sure of is that it agreed with the Bible because it was from the Bible!

This brings us back to I John 4:1 and testing the spirits; "Beloved, do not believe every spirit, but test the spirits to see whether they are from God; because many false prophets have gone out into the world." We must truly rely on the Holy Spirit to enable us to understand the Word, and to reveal God's truth to us as we need it, when we can understand it, and as we are equipped to properly utilize that truth. Testing every spirit who comes to guide me and inform me is not optional, because sometimes that friendly, helpful spirit is not from God. And if it is *not* from God, then it *is* from the devil! [Remember Eve and the serpent]

People are different, and some of us are more in tune with our feelings than are others. For those of us who do rely on feelings and intuition, being led and listening to the witness of the Spirit can easily be taken *too* far. No matter how God put us together, no matter what spiritual gifts we have or don't have, God's grace has given a single set of priorities for every Christian to follow in the study of His Word.

The work and the witness of the Spirit in the Christian's life is indispensable. If we are truly being led by the Holy Spirit, then we will be led to check on God's Word *first*, what the Church has taught historically *second*, and then we will look to the inner witness *last*. When our questions and doubts are satisfied and our minds and hearts acknowledge that what the Bible says is true and agree with what the Bible tells us to believe, then we can confidently say with Martin Luther, "***Here I stand; I can do no other***."

RECIPES FOR _IM_MATURITY

A pastor friend of mine likes to refer to the actual priorities of the average evangelical church as "*numbers, nickels, and noise*." Sadly, I have to agree with him.

Numbers means adding people to the membership rolls. A growing church is a spiritual church according to modern evangelical theory, so getting more folks into the pews becomes a top if not the number one priority. *How* we get them into our pews and try to keep them there is another story.

Ideally, numerical growth should result from evangelism and discipleship of the unsaved. Unfortunately, a lot of church growth these days is nothing more than thinly disguised *sheep-steeling* or *flock rotation*. Churches vie with each other for larger audiences. This competition with other churches leads to separation between them. After all, it is hard to cooperate with someone who is competing with you and stealing all your 'customers.'

In addition to separation from other churches, this also means competition in presenting a better, more polished and interesting worship service than the other guys. Special music, professional music groups, drama and special guest speakers are all part of the plans to increase attendance and grow larger and larger churches.

Part of the motivation for growing ever larger churches has led to the current mindset which is that if our church is growing, then this '*proves*' that God is with us and is blessing us. This unholy fascination with size is nothing more than a combination of *might makes right* and *the ends justify the means*. Any criticism of the current status quo in church activity is quickly squelched behind the self-righteous rational that God is blessing us with growth because we are doing the 'right' things. Does no one notice that this is saying that approval and acceptance is the earned result of our *own* 'righteous' behavior and practices? Is today's church so ignorant of the basic premises of grace that they can't even see that they are living under the very essence of the old covenant Law system?

Nickels refer to financial support for the church. Growing churches need a lot of money to pay for larger facilities with more seating, additional staff, and more sophisticated programs to attract larger numbers of supporters. Often, a lot of pressure will be exerted on the members, so that their giving increases. When it comes to money, guilt is frequently used to pry loose any extra change. Yet it was the church selling Papal Indulgences for the remission of some sins that infuriated Martin Luther and sparked the Protestant Reformation. When are we going to object?

Noise refers to the increasing number of programs and activities in the church to attract more *numbers*. The latest trends seem to revolve around the Praise and Worship service [rather than the pulpit] and the wearing of casual clothing to Church services, a trend being led by the pastors. Healing ministries, elaborate Sunday school facilities and functions, programs to attract families, high powered youth groups, home Bible studies, sermons with drama and films accompanying them and large, elaborate seasonal programs at Easter and Christmas; in short, anything that will attract large crowds and thereby draw in more *numbers*.

None of the things I have mentioned, numerical growth, financial support, or a variety of ministries is wrong or evil. However, making these things our *highest priorities* may be. In Hebrews 5:11-6:3 there is what should be seen as a stinging rebuke to many of these fast-growing super churches. We read; "Concerning him we have much to say, and it is hard to explain, since you have become dull of hearing. For though by this time you ought to be teachers, you have need again for some one to teach you the elementary principles of the oracles of God, and you have come to need milk and not solid food. For every one who partakes only of milk is not accustomed to the word of righteousness, for he is a babe. But solid food is for the mature, who because of practice have their senses trained to discern [not determine] good and evil. Therefore leaving the elementary teaching about the Christ, let us press on to maturity, not laying again a foundation of repentance from dead works and of faith toward God, of instruction about washings, and laying on of hands, and the resurrection of the dead, and eternal judgment. And this we shall do, if God permits."

GRADUATING FROM NURSERY SCHOOL

The reason many evangelical churches should find this to be a stinging rebuke is because truly *mature* Christians are a *rarity* in their memberships. For the most part, these huge churches are nothing more than spiritual nurseries, a state being perpetuated by the lack of depth and quality in their discipling, teaching and preaching. They have many spiritual babes who are accustomed to drinking only milk, because that is all they are ever served. Those that do grow in these environments are the exceptions, not the rule.

Looking at Hebrews 6:1-2, what is being identified as *elementary teachings*? The first one is ". . . *repentance from dead works and of faith toward God.*" Isn't this the most basic gospel message one could preach? Does not this theme dominate most of the sermons we hear every Sunday in evangelical churches across the land? My answer in both cases is **yes**!

Repentance and faith are two of the fundamental components of an evangelistic message. But how many of those listening to these sermons every Sunday morning are already saved and do not need to be evangelized? What would you guess; ninety to ninety five percent? If that's true, and I believe it is very close, than 90 to 95 percent of the sermons are being directed to only five to ten percent of the audience. This also means that ninety to ninety five percent of the people there on Sunday Morning are *not* being fed anything more nutritious than a baby's diet of milk.

Looking at the other *elementary teachings* referred to in this passage, we come to ". . . *instruction about washings.*" Remember that most if not all of those reading this letter are Jewish Christians, raised under the Jewish Laws. Obviously they would need explanations about why the Jewish Ceremonial Laws were no longer in force.

When my Gentile brain thinks about *washings* in a spiritual context, I usually associate it with *water baptism*. How much wind has been expelled from our pulpits about the necessity of being baptized, and which is the proper mode for baptizing; sprinkling, pouring, or immersing? Yet Hebrews is calling this an elementary teaching we need to grow beyond!

Next the ". . .*laying on of hands*" is mentioned. This brings to mind the miracle healing services some Christians feel are so necessary. Yet many of these miracle healing services have been exposed as fraudulent, and about the only thing learned at these events is misinformation about the nature of faith and God's will with regard to health. Let's move on!

The last thing mentioned in this list of elementary teachings the church *must* move past if we are to have a mature body of Christians representing our Lord in this world today is, " . . . *resurrection of the dead and eternal judgment*." The study of future events prophesied in the Bible is called *eschatology*. One of the best selling books written on this subject is Hal Lindsey's *The Late Great Planet Earth*, which is all about what Biblical prophecy says is going to happen. Of course, it doesn't hurt Christians to study eschatology, but it has very little to do with maturing baby Christians. So, let's keep moving on.

TEACHING TOWARDS MATURITY

One of the great mistakes being made today concerns the assumption in most evangelical churches that *evangelism* must take place from the pulpit. Many believe that a Church service without an invitation to be saved is not only inappropriate, but even downright unbiblical. Such people do not realize that the practice of offering invitations at the end of the service is a fairly recent practice, popularized by revivalist Charles G. Finney (1792-1875). I do wonder how they explain conversions prior to the 19th Century.

In keeping with this evangelical fervor, Christians are constantly encouraged [or pestered] to witness and lead the unsaved to Christ. Realistically, they also know that no matter how much their congregations are encouraged [or badgered] to share their faith it just doesn't produce the kind of results they are looking for.

Consequently the pulpit becomes the main arena for salvation. This in turn demands that sermons be simple and understandable to the unsaved. However, most churches are filled with believers. The result is that 95% of evangelical sermons are directed to maybe 5% of the congregation. The other 95% of the congregation soon begins to feel the spiritual starvation that results from a consistent diet of spiritual 'milk.'

What amazes me is that they don't seem to realize what is happening or why. Actually, if you want Christians to mature then you must feed them spiritual 'meat.' If Churches won't teach the Christians under their care with the express purpose of *maturing* them, then their assumptions are pretty much correct. Babies are hardly equipped to produce and care for more babies! If only we would just take our priorities from Scripture, we would see a great upsurge in evangelism, if not a full-fledged revival, because all the Christians would be engaged in evangelism *effectively*.

Chapter Three
ARE WE DEAD OR JUST WOUNDED?

LOSING THE HUMAN RACE

Losing the human race can be looked at in two ways. On the one hand, we humans are always racing around desperately trying to find meaning and fulfillment in our lives; and failing! The failure to find meaning and fulfillment in one's life is definitely losing the 'race.'

At the same time, the Bible warns us that apart from Jesus Christ, the human race is lost, separated from God by sin. This certainly counts as losing the race, too. Actually they are very tightly connected. Failure to find meaning in life is the direct result of failing to find Jesus Christ. Either way we come at the problem of finding meaning, fulfillment, and salvation, God's gift of grace is the only way to win the human race.

The gift of God's grace offers us much more than just 'fire insurance.'[3] Grace is not simply about avoiding hell, it is about discovering a whole new way of life in and with Jesus. In the first chapter, we discussed The Gift, which is the grace of God. Concerning this gift of grace, it was stated that grace is the most important, essential subject we could ever study, because grace is not just the central truth of the Bible; it is also the *key* to unlocking and understanding the entire Bible. Grace is true life. Apart from grace lies certain death: it matters not whether one is breathing or not. Before one seeks the gift of grace, they must be convinced of the need for grace.

There are two ways to establish the importance and the true value of God's grace. First, the importance and value of God's grace to you or me is determined by how badly we need it. We give little thought to the *value* of a glass of water from the faucet in the kitchen. But if we found ourselves lost in the Sahara dessert, dying of thirst, a drink of water would be the one thing we valued the most. Value is always determined by one's greed or need!

The other way to establish the importance and especially the true value of God's grace is to consider just how expensive it was to procure. There is no cost to us for God's grace; it is given freely. However, the cost to God to establish grace for us was the sacrifice of His only unique Son, Jesus Christ, on the cross at Calvary.

This puts the intrinsic value of grace far beyond comparison or even comprehension. Considering the actual value of grace to you and me, it would seem to be a valuable use of our time to discuss just how deeply we need grace. We need to understand how lost we all are, how the human race got lost in the first place, and what God and His grace can do about it.

RACING AFTER FULFILLMENT

Every human being wants to find and experience fulfillment. Consequently, finding fulfillment is the primary motive for why we are all running. Now there are a lot of different ideas about what will fulfill humans. Many assume fulfillment comes from acquiring things, whether it is money, power, fame or more toys. Some seek fulfillment by trying to become more desirable outwardly. They worship at the altars of outer beauty and physical fitness. Others believe they will find fulfillment either by rejecting society (by *dropping out*) or by trying to reform society or at least some aspects of it (with things like Marxism or environmentalism).

Some of us discover that we are not going to win this race on our own. Others think they have already won the race but life will eventually prove them to be very sadly mistaken. Some will even seek to avoid the pain of losing through drugs, alcohol, gluttony, or promiscuity. A fortunate remnant will discover that no human can win the race by themselves and they will turn to God.

Christians expect to find fulfillment through living the Christian life *successfully*. While this is true, most Christians do not clearly understand what a successful Christian life looks like. Those who fail to acquire a correct picture of Christian success will sooner or later think they are losing this race too. One of the lessons we Christians need to learn is that our standards of measurement are vastly different from God's. Man judges according to law; God judges by grace!

Consequently, we need to learn an entirely different way of looking at and living our daily lives. As we are clearly told in Scripture, we believers are not under the Law but under grace. Some Christians will discover the fulfillment of living by grace through faith. The rest will strive and fail, resulting in putting themselves on the sidelines. They hope that they will get to heaven someday, and indeed they will, but they will also miss a lot on the journey.

EVOLUTION VERSUS CREATION

Discovering the extreme value of grace and why it is so absolutely necessary to us starts way back at the beginning with the origins of man. Having an intelligent discussion about the true origin of man has been made increasingly difficult due to the emphasis on evolution being the only 'true' answer to man's origins. Moreover, for many the existence of God is either passively ignored or actively rejected. Either way, God, grace, faith, and salvation have become archaic terms and useless concepts to a great many modern so-called sophisticated members of the human race [also known as secular humanists].

This does not mean religion is dead. No sir, not at all. Many people today still practice some form of religion. The problem is that what many are practicing bears little if any resemblance to *Biblical Christianity*. Some religious leaders today actually believe and teach that Christianity is harmful to the success and fulfillment of the human race.

We are definitely living in a *post*-Christian culture. This has been a fairly recent development when compared against the recorded history of the human race. Since we humans can not exist in a vacuum, physically, intellectually, morally, or spiritually, what has evolved to replace belief in God and the Bible is something called *secular humanism*. It really is a catch-all term for everything that is not biblically Christian. A secular humanist may be someone who is religious, agnostic, or a confirmed atheist. In any event, secular humanists are surely lost.

Whatever the case may be, they all hold certain beliefs in common. *Secular* simply means anyone or anything that is *not* concerned with God. It refers to all things material and worldly and consequently attaches significance *only* to these worldly, material things.

Humanism believes in an ever shifting, human-based morality, and is only concerned with the current needs, desires, and interests of humans. Consequently, it is a system of thought that is based on the values, characteristics, and behavior that are believed to be best in human beings, rather than on any supernatural authority or divine revelation.[4]

Obviously, when the secular mind encounters the question of man's origins and purpose for existence, an answer must be found that is well outside the realm of revealed Biblical truth. For example, to satisfy this need, secular minds have latched onto the theory of evolution to explain human existence. Humans are merely a more highly evolved animal who supposedly trace their origins back to lesser life forms. Unknowingly, by advocating evolution, secular humanists are declaring themselves to be nothing more important than a *fortuitous accident* that has descended from other animals.

The widely embraced theory of evolution leads to some major social problems. The problems are obvious even if the real cause is not. As secularism evolves, it leads to all sorts of increasingly serious problems with morality, character, and conduct. More and more families are being decimated by selfishness and self-centeredness, leading to a rapidly increasing divorce rate on the one hand and a declining interest in the necessity and sanctity of marriage on the other.

Abortions abound, justified as a woman's right to choose, yet some still call it murder. The conflict over the right to choose against the right to life springs directly from which theory we hold regarding the origin of man. Were we created or are we evolved? What is decided here affects how humanity views such social issues as abortion, euthanasia, medical ethics and priorities, care for the elderly and the handicapped, and in general, society's moral standards or lack of them. What you and I hold to be true about our origins will have a decided affect on our entire lives.

THE CASE FOR CREATION

In order to embrace the theory of evolution, the modern secular humanist has to ignore some very compelling evidence concerning man's origin as a being created by God. If you are going to believe in creation, then you're going to have to believe in a Creator. God would be the best [and only] choice for Creator in my opinion.

The evidence for the existence of God is found both within people [internal evidence] and in the world which surrounds us [external evidence]. For example, in the New Testament, Romans 1:18-19 clearly states, "For the wrath of God is revealed from heaven against all ungodliness and unrighteousness of men, who suppress the truth in unrighteousness, because that which is known about God is evident within them; for God made it evident to them. For since the creation of the world His invisible attributes, His eternal power and divine nature, have been clearly seen, being understood through what has been made, so that they are without excuse." The real reason for natural man wanting to avoid acknowledging the existence of God may have much more to do with a human's unavoidable sense of guilt over sin and their justifiable fear of God's wrath, than with any so-called 'scientific' theories.

For anyone who is willing to make an open minded investigation into the possibility of God's existence, they will find plenty of convincing evidence *in nature* without ever having to open a Bible. Some of the most compelling evidence for creation is found in the fossil record. There is also some pretty convincing evidence of the existence of God inside each one of us.

Romans 1:18-23 says there is compelling physical or external evidence for the existence of God! For example, consider how beautifully balanced nature is, and how easily we humans upset that balance, no matter how well intentioned we may be. Consider the miraculous complexity of the human body. The brain, heart, lungs, and other vital organs are all mounted inside a rigid framework called the skeleton, with muscles, nerves, tendons, and cartilage holding it all together and enabling it to function, not to mention the circulatory system, nervous system, and even the body's ability to heal itself.

Let's face it; we are truly unique and amazing creations. Yet 'modern science' wants us to believe we evolved from some simple, single cell creatures through a process of random selection and elimination. One has to wonder why the secular mind would reduce this marvel of creation to nothing more than a random, fortuitous series of accidents called evolution.

Although the theory of evolution is offered as a rational substitute for the Biblical account of creation and explanation of man's origins and existence, it is interesting that none of these brilliant, scientific evolutionists can satisfactorily explain why the fossil records contain no transitional life forms. Nor can these 'experts' explain the sudden and simultaneous appearance of multiple, complex life forms in the fossil record.

In point of fact, the physical archaeological evidence supports the 'theory' of creation, and that life was created in a brief period of time. Why isn't it possible that a God who could create all life, do so in six literal 24 hour days, and not the billions of years that the evolutionists claim natural selection took.

There is also some very compelling internal evidence to indicate that we humans are a good deal more than just a genetic joke. For one thing, humans cannot help being moral creatures, which clearly sets us apart from all other created beings. Humans have a conscience; animals do not. Humans have self-awareness and the ability to reflect on their conduct; animals do not because they are instinctive. Animals kill other animals over territorial claims, to gain a mate, and for food, without an ounce of remorse, again as a matter of instinct.

To be sure, humans kill for noble reasons, such as to defend themselves, protect their lands and home, and of course to protect their families. However, humans also kill other humans over jealousy, greed, and hatred. And, with the exception of the sociopath, humans feel remorse over their wicked deeds, but even remorse and guilt do not slow them down.

The real question the theory of evolution needs to satisfactorily answer is where do our consciences and morality come from if we are nothing more than evolved animals that supposedly live by instinct? At the same time how can evolution explain how we, as ascending animals in the evolutionary scheme, have also become more sadistic and barbaric than our so-called lesser 'cousins?' Only man continually invents more efficient methods for taking the lives of others.

Speaking of morality, sociologists tell us that murder is a universally forbidden crime. Every tribe on earth gives evidence of having standards of right and wrong, and murder is one that is always wrong. This fact correlates perfectly with the Biblical account of the fall of all humanity. One of the consequences of disobeying God was that humanity acquired the knowledge of good and evil, making it possible for man to not only construct moral codes, but to also know how to violate those codes. This is something no animal including our pet poodles has ever had to be concerned about.

Along with some form of moral code it also seems that every tribe that has ever existed, to our knowledge, has practiced some form of religion. Some worship nature, making images of beasts or birds from wood or stone. Others worship the sun, the stars, or the moon. The Greeks and later the Romans believed in a whole pantheon of Gods, endowed with all of the human weaknesses, and devised all manner of interesting tales about them. Some have sought to placate their versions of God with sacrifices, including living human ones. There is abundant evidence that the human race has moral concerns and is also incurably religious, while at the same time busily demonstrating a truly failed sense of morality.

We humans have the ability to think, imagine, create, invent, feel, love, hate, make judgments, show compassion and forgive. According to Genesis 1:27 this is because, "God created man in His own image, in the image of God He created them; male and female He created them." Where else could these qualities come from, if not from God in whose image we are created?

EVERY DESIGN DEMANDS A DESIGNER

The sun, the moon, the stars, the forests, plains, and seas and our unique humanity, all bear testimony to an intelligent design. Moreover, doesn't common sense and nature teach us that every intelligent design demands an Intelligent Designer? So who is this Intelligent Designer if not God?

Furthermore, if we can agree to believe in an Intelligent Designer whom we call God then why wouldn't it be reasonable to believe that this God provided us with a reliable document called the Bible! In the Bible, God explains Who He is, who and what we are, what He wants for us and from us, and what we need for the journey, along with enough information to insure that we will be able to understand and function usefully in this life before spending eternity with Him.

Why isn't it reasonable to believe that the Bible is entirely the Word of God? We know the Bible was revealed to us through some 42 authors writing over a period of approximately 1,500 years without contradictions. No other piece of literature has ever accomplished complete unanimity with this many authors let alone over this spread of time.

The Bible has been transmitted to us through copying and translation in such a way that even today we can be assured that it remains the accurate and completely reliable Word of God, and this accuracy has been established through purely secular literary and scholarly methods.

To believe in Christ Jesus is to believe in the existence of God. Despite the negative influences and the misleading, erroneous beliefs surrounding us, I submit that belief in a personal, caring, and loving God is intellectually, scientifically, historically, and practically reasonable, and it will turn out to be the most reasonable thing any human could ever believe.

AUTHENTIC CHRISTIANITY

Down through the centuries, there have been enough religious charlatans to give Christianity a bad name in the minds of many. For example, we have all heard the criticism that Christians are all *hypocrites*.

A hypocrite is anyone whose actions and conduct fall below the standards *they claim* to believe and practice. Since all Christians are less than perfect, if we went around claiming to be perfect, or saying that to become a Christian you must become perfect, *then* the charge of hypocrisy against Christians would be valid.

Now I am not a perfect Christian and I have never met a perfect Christian. But when we say "Please be patient, God is not finished with me yet," then we are just being honest. This is not hypocrisy; this is reality.

There are many people who would be deeply offended if you told them they are *not* Christians. This is because many people have mistakenly concluded that being a Christian refers to a person's conduct, rather than to what they believe and frankly, *Who* they know. To them, demonstrating qualities such as *kindness*, *goodness*, and *morality*, is what defines a true Christian. To imply they are not Christians because they do not believe in Christ insults their sense of goodness, integrity and morality. It is the same as calling them evil and immoral.

Other people assume they are Christians because they are not something else. They reason that if they are not Buddhist, Muslim, Jewish, or Pagan, then they must be Christians as if one becomes a Christian by default. And let's not forget those poor, misguided souls called atheists who claim to be deeply offended at the mere mention of God or Christianity, let alone the displaying of uniquely Christian symbols or objects such as the nativity at Christmas.

Authentic Christianity has been constantly under attack since its inception over 2,000 years ago. Christianity has been assailed as a stupid superstition, a crutch for the weak minded, and even as a danger to the general welfare of mankind. There are a growing number of voices who actually think Christianity should be banned, even though this has never worked before.

Some people think the Bible teaches it's adherents to be bigoted, narrow minded, and cruel. Unfortunately, sometimes this is true, although it most certainly is not Biblical. Consequently, the only way to make a fair assessment of Christianity is to go to the Bible, actually read the Bible and study what it really says. One has to wonder why most of Christianity's critics never bother with *due diligence*.

If we want to present a realistic authentic Christian Faith to the world, then it would help to know what a real, authentic Christian is. According to the Bible, an authentic Christian *believes* that Jesus Christ is the true, divine Son of God, who came to earth to reveal to us what God the Father is really like, and to actually pay the penalty for our sins by dying on the Cross. Authentic Christians also believe that Christ was literally raised from the dead and shortly thereafter ascended back to heaven. Authentic Christians believe that only God is worthy of our worship and devotion, and that God and His will should always be our first priority.

An authentic Christian knows that pleasing God judicially has already happened at the cross. Jesus Christ has already paid the price for their sins. Moreover, they know that their faith in Christ has been reckoned to them as righteousness. Pleasing God is the result of placing our faith and trust in Him in our daily experience. Authentic Christians know that "without faith it is impossible to please Him, for he who comes to God must believe that He is, and that He is a rewarder of those who seek Him [Hebrews 11:6]."

Authentic Christians believe the Bible is the Word of God. This does not mean an authentic Christian knows everything in the Bible. However, if we believe the Bible is God's Word, then authentic Christians are going to believe what it says as they have opportunity to learn it. This is why authentic Christians are also called believers. [See Romans 6:5-11; Romans 10:8-11; I Corinthians 15:1-4].

Knowing, believing, and putting your trust in these essential basics is what makes someone an authentic Christian. The proof of true or saving faith rests completely on one's belief in who Jesus is and what He has done! Baptism, communion, church attendance, giving and good works all have their place, but the cross and Christ's death, burial, and resurrection are the only basis for salvation and life, and are the acts of grace that are the heart and substance of the Christian Faith.

There will always be those who represent themselves to be Christians, if for no other reason than they believe they are leading good moral lives. Good conduct is always of value to an authentic Christian in this life, but authentic Christians also realize their conduct will never rise to the perfect Biblical level in this life. Authentic Christians are not perfect, and they know this. More importantly, authentic Christians firmly believe that all of their sins, past, present and future are forgiven at the cross through the shed blood of Jesus Christ our Savior. Since authentic Christians know they are accepted and approved of by God, they are not forced to make themselves out to be something they are not. This is why authentic Christians are *not* hypocrites!

TROUBLE IN PARADISE

The Garden of Eden was a real place and Adam and Eve were real people. They were the first two human beings to live on earth and consequently all other humans are descended from them. The Garden is believed to have been located somewhere near the Persian Gulf in what is now southeastern Iraq. The events that occurred there and their consequences are also real and have affected every human being since the first family. These are not myths!

The problem Jesus Christ came to solve permanently was the sin Adam bequeathed to all of his descendents. Jesus solved this problem by His death on the cross and through His resurrection and ascension into heaven.

The first time evil is mentioned in the Bible is in Genesis 2:9 where it is used in the description of a specific tree in the center of the Garden of Eden known as the "tree of the knowledge of good and evil." There was another tree, the "tree of life," in the center of the Garden, and from this tree the first couple could and should have eaten, but didn't. In fact, God commanded Adam and Eve to eat of the fruit of any tree in the Garden of Eden except the fruit from the "tree of the knowledge of good and evil."

Throughout history, the planet Earth and every generation to live upon it has had to contend with the consequences of sin. Sin has accompanied the development of the human race in the form of strife, wars, pestilence, disease, immorality, poverty, crimes of every kind, slavery, and always the fearsome specter of death. All of this resulted from just one act of disobedience.

The only good news coming out of that giant fiasco is that since one man's [Adam] sin spread to all, in all fairness it would only take one Man's [Jesus] act of sacrificial obedience to cancel out the consequences of the original sin. You can read about the original sin and the fall of the human race in the Bible book of Genesis, chapters 2 and 3, and you can read all about how this divine 'fairness' doctrine works in Romans 5:12-21.

The significance of this forbidden tree in the garden was not in the fruit it bore, because the fruit itself caused no harm. Rather it was the act of disobeying God that would strip them of their innocence and make them forever conscious of both good and evil.

The saddest part of their disobedience was that they only had that one command to obey. Genesis 2:16-17 says, "And the Lord God commanded the man, saying, 'From any tree of the garden you may eat freely; but from the tree of the knowledge of good and evil you shall not eat, for in that day that you eat from it you shall surely die.'"

The way Satan managed to tempt Eve was fairly simple. First, he told her *part* of the *truth*, the part she would want to hear. At the same time Satan was manipulating Eve by using her natural inborn desire to be a better person. According to Abraham Maslow's hierarchy of human needs, the ultimate need of humans is "self-actualization," which basically means we want to be the best possible person we can be. Satan was offering Eve and Adam equal standing with God, which is as good as it gets!

When Satan got to the warning God gave Adam and Eve, he simply contradicted it. Of course what Satan was really offering Eve, and through her, Adam, was the *perception* of power and control. Genesis 3:4-5 tells us that the devil said; "You shall surely not die! For God knows that in the day you eat from it your eyes will be opened [knowledge], and you will be like God, knowing good and *evil* [implying they would be in control of their lives]."

Satan was correct when he told Eve that the knowledge of both good and evil would make them **feel** equal to God. What Satan did not tell them is that they could never handle this kind of knowledge because God never created them to be able to do so in the first place. Jesus warned us of this misperception in John 15 by telling us to continually abide in Him, for apart from Him, we can do nothing!

ORIGINAL SIN

What God always intended for humans, and still does, is that we trust Him completely, depend on Him completely, and consequently be able to obey Him completely. However, when mankind takes the bit in their mouth because they think they have been elevated to a position equal to God, we humans no longer see the need to trust in and depend upon God. We humans have made the monumental mistake of believing we are adequate and capable of obeying God through the exercise of that little thing we call our *free* will.

When Adam and Eve *disobeyed* God, their one act of disobedience or *sin* resulted in their eyes being opened. All of a sudden they were fully aware of the existence of both good and evil. What was worse, along with this new found knowledge came awareness that there are significant *consequences* for *disobedience*. It is doubtful that Adam and Eve fully grasped the significance of death, but the fact that they tried to hide from God when they heard Him coming certainly indicates their awareness of a serious consequence for disobeying God.

The disobedience of Adam and Eve and its consequence is called the *Original Sin*. The impact of their disobedience on all their descendents is referred to as the *fall* of man. Their one act of disobedience opened a veritable Pandora's Box of *sin* and loosed it into our world. This *fall* guaranteed that *every* human being born into this world would be fatally 'infected' by sin. All of us are descended from Adam and Eve and have therefore inherited this knowledge of good and evil along with the instinctual fear of punishment.

Along with God's command to not eat the fruit of this one specific tree, He also warned the first couple that disobedience to His command carried with it the promise of certain *death*. God told Adam and Eve the *truth* about *sin* and *death*; so why didn't they just obey Him? It is one thing to know and understand the truth; obviously it is quite another to obey or do the truth. It's no wonder that in general, the human race wants to avoid God at all costs.

THE TRUTH ABOUT TRUTH

Because sin entered our world, being created in the image and likeness of God does not mean we automatically have spiritual understanding. I Corinthians 2:14 explains that "...a natural man does not accept the things of the Spirit of God; for they are foolishness to him, and he cannot understand them, because they are spiritually appraised."

The easiest way to avoid embarrassment over an idea or belief we do not understand is to ridicule and trivialize it. This is why we read in I Corinthians 1:21-25, "For since in the wisdom of God the world through its wisdom did not come to know God, God was well pleased through the foolishness of the message preached to save those who believe. For indeed Jews ask for signs, and Greeks search for wisdom; but we preach Christ crucified, to Jews a stumbling block, and to Gentiles foolishness, but to those who are the called, both Jews and Greeks, Christ the power of God and the wisdom of God. Because the foolishness of God is wiser than men, and the weakness of God is stronger than men."

We Christians also struggle with some of the deeper spiritual aspects of Christianity, but for a very different reason. The reason behind this problem is explained in I Corinthians 3:1-3; "And I, brethren, could not speak to you as to spiritual [spiritually mature] men, but as to men of flesh, as to babes in Christ. I gave you milk to drink, not solid food; for you were not yet able to receive it. Indeed, even now you are not able, for you are still fleshly. For since there is jealousy and strife amongst you, are you not fleshly, and are you not walking like mere men?" Biblical education is indispensible to spiritual growth and maturity and spiritual growth and maturity is indispensible to learning ever deeper spiritual truths.

One thing we must never forget is that the Christian faith is a living, dynamic *process*, not just an event. It is always possible to acquire 'head' knowledge, but head knowledge never reaches and changes hearts. God wants us to *know* the truth, at the same time realizing that knowing the truth is not simply collecting and remembering facts.

God's idea of knowing the truth is to become *personally acquainted* with the Truth, because ultimately, the Truth is a living reality found in a singularly unique Person, Jesus Christ the Son of God with whom we are to interact on a daily basis. John 14:6 affirms this by quoting Jesus; "Jesus said to him, 'I am the way, and the truth, and the life; no one comes to the Father, but through Me.'"

Because knowing the Truth is absolutely essential, Satan puts a great deal of effort into stretching the truth, twisting the truth, and outright denying the truth in order to deceive us, mislead us, and manipulate us. The only thing Satan can be trusted to do is to try to control us, prevent us, destroy us, or neutralize us! The oddest part of this scenario is that by far, the devil is humanity's worst enemy. Yet somehow Satan has managed to blind humanity for the most part and trick them into not even believing that he exists! How is that for a strategy! And it works as long as Satan can find ways to keep us from studying, understanding and living God's Word.

To defeat Satan in his work against humanity, God gives us His Spirit and the Bible to enlighten us about sin; where it comes from, what it is, who is behind it, how it affects us and why it persists. God explains to us about the fall of man and Original Sin. He informs us that because of Original Sin, we are born into this world separated from God. He warns us that being born with a sinful nature makes life painful and hard and leads to death and Hell. God tells us that being born in Sin means we are born already spiritually dead. And if we are already spiritually dead, how can we do anything about our lost condition?

THE TRUTH ABOUT DEATH

God warned Adam and Eve that if they disobeyed Him, they would surely die. Romans 6:23a warns us, "For the wages of sin is death." It was true in the beginning and it is still true now! However, when we try to warn our friends and neighbors that the wages of sin is death, usually they will look at us strangely and try to avoid us, or scorn and laugh at us, and sometimes become instantly hostile towards us. What they won't do is believe us. Why they won't believe us is because they can't; they are, just as God told us, *spiritually dead*.

This is exactly what Ephesians 2:1 is referring to when it says, "And you were dead in your trespasses and sins…" This is an accurate description of the natural state of secular mankind but try getting them to believe it. The reason is that all spiritual truths are spiritually appraised. Regardless of how hard we try, only God can awaken a dead soul and breathe into them the Spirit of life and faith, and cause them to believe the truth. This is why conversion is described as regeneration which means being born again from above.

Being dead in our trespasses and sins does not mean we have stopped breathing or ceased to exist, but it does mean we are dead, because God says we are dead! What we have to do now is figure out from the Scriptures what God is talking about.

First off, we know that according to God there are *two* kinds of death. There is *physical death* when our living soul leaves our physical bodies, which immediately begins to decompose. Then there is *spiritual death*, which we know a good deal less about than we know about *physical death*.

Nevertheless, God has told us that spiritual death, not physical death, is the most serious result of the *fall* and *Original Sin*! Jesus clearly says in Matthew 10:28, "And do not fear those who kill the body [i.e., physical death], but are unable to kill the soul [i.e. spiritual death]; but rather fear Him who is able to destroy both soul and body in Hell."

All of us, because of Adam and Eve's original sin, are born into a world and dwell among a people who are completely separated from God, even though some seem to be very religious. When the Scriptures say the wages of sin is death or that we are dead in our trespasses and sins, it is referring to the fact that the entire human race is born separated from God. Speaking to Christians, the Apostle Paul says in Ephesians 2:3, "Among them we too all formerly lived in the lusts of our flesh, indulging [or doing] the desires of the flesh and of the mind, and were by nature children of wrath, even as the rest."

Because Adam and Eve failed to obey God, sin was admitted into our world, separating everyone in every generation from God. This is spiritual death, and it is by far the harshest death. In addition to being separated from God, all who are born into our world will also eventually die physically, but they will not cease to exist. Life once created, never ceases to exist. What physical death accomplishes then is separation from our earthly physical bodies. Our problem is not eternal existence, but rather where we will spend eternity.

Whether God is talking to us about death in the literal physical sense or about death in the literal spiritual sense always be assured that when the Scriptures refer to death, whether physical or spiritual, the death it is always referring to is *separation*. In the Bible, death never means *cessation*! We will all live forever; sadly, not everyone will live eternally in the saving grace of God.

NO, NOT EVEN ONE

Although God has provided us with a way of escaping the consequences of sin through Jesus Christ, the majority of the human race will reject the offer. Humans naturally reject the need for salvation because it means giving up the right to control their lives. This they will not do for they are not even able to do so.

Nevertheless, we are told that God still loves us. Romans 5:6-10 says that Christ died for helpless, ungodly sinners as a demonstration of God's love for us, and He did this while we were God's enemies. Nevertheless, apart from His gift of grace and faith, we will reject Him.

Clearly there is something wrong with us. Romans 3:23 says "...all have sinned and fall short of the glory of God ..." Romans 6:23a says, "...the wages of sin is death, but the free gift of God is eternal life in Christ Jesus our Lord." Still we reject Him.

All humans reject God automatically because of their fallen nature. This is the sad result of original sin and the fall of humanity. Romans 3:10-12 clearly describes natural man's state of mind with regard to God and righteousness:

"There is none righteous, not even one;
There is none who understands,
There is none who seeks for God;
All have turned aside, together they have become useless;
There is none who does good,
There is not even one."

According to God, no one is righteous, no one understands these things we have just been looking at, no one naturally seeks God, every one of us has turned aside, away from God, every one of us has become completely useless to God, no one does good, not even one! Romans 5:6-10 further identifies us as helpless, ungodly sinners and enemies of God.

A lot of people, including many Christians, want to disagree with the conclusions of this passage in Romans. They argue that there are many people who mean well and are seeking to do good to the best of their ability. Moreover, they almost always know stories about someone who spent years searching for God. This passage does not deny that there are always people seeking a rewarding religious experience. The point being made in Romans 3 is that no human naturally seeks after the true God and His salvation. Any authentic seekers are those who have first been drawn!

The Apostle Paul had this to say about his own Jewish kinsmen in Romans 10:2-3; "For I bear them witness that they have a zeal for God, but not in accordance with knowledge. For not knowing about God's righteousness, and seeking to establish their own, they did not subject themselves to the righteousness of God."

Because of original sin, our fallen human nature always seeks after what we determine to be in our own best interests. Our own fallen natures have turned us in on ourselves to seek answers. Natural man has absolutely no interest in how God sees things or what God has to say. No one naturally seeks authentic Christianity. Therefore, when we do encounter someone who seems to be looking in the right places in the right way, we need to give the credit to God and the fact that His Spirit is drawing this person in the right direction.

WHERE CONFUSION REIGNS

It begins with our limited knowledge and understanding of both God and our selves. We compound this problem by subjecting and verifying the truth of God's Word against what makes sense to us. When there are obvious differences between God's revelation and what makes sense to us, our natural instinct is to attempt to explain God's Words by clothing them with secular reasoning. Instead of rejecting our cherished beliefs (based on instincts and secularism) when God says they are wrong, we look for ways to camouflage and explain away God's truth.

The first and what should be the most obvious conclusion we should reach, is that if God is telling the truth, which we are trying to rationalize and explain away then our reaction only proves that our human understanding of spiritual things is sadly deficient. We do not have the luxury of deciding what is good or evil, because our so-called understanding is based on superficial observations and speculations and is fueled by self-centered desires. If God's Word is true, then there can be no doubt that secular humanity is really lost and dead in their sins and trespasses. If God's Word is true, it means we are completely incapable of doing or saying anything that would save us.

For this reason, Jesus informed the disciples about the difficulty of being saved in Matthew 19:25-26. "And when the disciples heard this, they were very astonished and said, 'Then who can be saved?' And looking upon them Jesus said to them, 'With men this is impossible, but with God all things are possible.'" Please notice that Jesus did not say salvation would be difficult; He said that apart from God it was *impossible*!

We would all do well to meditate on some of these pearls of wisdom from the Book of Proverbs: "Trust in the Lord with all your heart, and do not lean on your own understanding. In all your ways acknowledge Him, and He will make your paths straight. Do not be wise in your own eyes; fear the Lord and turn away from evil [3:5-7]." "Commit your works to the Lord, and your plans will be established. The Lord has made everything for its own purpose, even the wicked for the day of evil [16:3-4]." "The mind of man plans his way, but the Lord direct his steps [16:9]." "There is a way which seems right to a man, but its end is the way of death [16:25]."

It should be obvious from this brief collection of passages that our thoughts and opinions come in as a distant second to the revealed wisdom and will of God in the Scriptures.

DEAD OR JUST WOUNDED?

When it comes to answering the question of how a lost sinner is saved, we Christians tend to speak out of both sides of our mouth. If we are asked is their anything we can do to earn our salvation, our answer is absolutely nothing; salvation is given as a free gift of God's grace. However, when we are asked what we must do to be saved, we get a variety of answers, none of which is "absolutely nothing but believe." The most common response given by Evangelicals is that we must "pray to receive Christ as our Lord and Savior." However, John 1:11-13 explains, "He came to His own [the Jews], and those who were His own did not receive Him. But as many as received Him [Jews or Gentiles], to them He gave the right to become children of God, even to those who believe in His name, who were born, not of blood nor of the will of the flesh nor of the will of man, but of God." It appears from this passage that receiving and believing are equivalent.

Romans 10:8-13, 17 also bears out this close relationship between believing and receiving. "But what does it say? 'THE WORD IS NEAR

YOU, IN YOUR MOUTH AND IN YOUR HEART'–that is, the word of faith which we are preaching, that if you confess with your mouth Jesus as Lord, and believe in your heart that God raised Him from the dead, you will be saved; for with the heart a person believes, resulting in righteousness, and with the mouth he confesses, resulting in salvation. For the Scripture says, 'WHOEVER BELIEVES IN HIM WILL NOT BE DISAPPOINTED.' For there is no distinction between Jew and Greek; for the same Lord is Lord of all, abounding in riches for all who call on Him; for 'WHOEVER WILL CALL ON THE NAME OF THE LORD WILL BE SAVED.'"

Obviously prayer is a valid means of receiving Christ as Lord and Savior, nevertheless belief initiated faith is the most essential component. Romans 10:17 states, "So faith comes from hearing, and hearing by the word of Christ." Tragically, in many cases other conditions for salvation are added.

For example, some tell us we must go forward at the invitation given in a church service. Most prominent in this group are the Evangelicals who insist that any church which does not offer a public invitation to accept Christ at the end of every worship service is not a valid, Bible believing and teaching church. Apparently those holding these views are not aware that churches did not begin giving invitations until this method was introduced by the evangelist C.G. Finney in the early 19th Century. Their point of view leaves one wondering how they would explain salvation occurring prior to the 19th Century.

Some will say we must be baptized by full immersion, while others insist that we demonstrate the baptism of the Holy Spirit with speaking in tongues. In any of these examples and in fact as a doctrinal mainstay of the modern Evangelical Church Movement, the central criteria for salvation is that one must *choose* to be saved by *choosing* to accept Christ as Lord and Savior. Of course this position is maintained while blithely ignoring the repeated Biblical injunction is to *believe* in the Lord Jesus Christ, not choose!

Some theologians believe this choosing by exercising one's free will borders on a salvation by works of the flesh, while many others maintain that on a practical level, our salvation is a joint effort between God and us. Generally speaking, most of today's Christians do not have a problem with the idea that our salvation is indeed a joint effort. The reason many of us do not have any objections springs from the contemporary problem of Biblical ignorance and secular camouflage.

One of the contributors to Biblical ignorance results from how we react to controversy. It seems that a new priority is emerging among Christians and it is that we *avoid anything* that might cause division among the members of the body of Christ. Perhaps this could be called the new *Evangelical Ecumenical Movement.* Trying to promote unity between different Christian groups or friendly relations with different religions may seem a noble cause, but the first casualty of such efforts always seems to be the revealed Word of God recorded in the Bible.

The problem with this approach is that it eventually leads to treating any and every topic of debate or disagreement as divisive and is therefore to be avoided or ignored. Sooner or later this attitude over the evils of division results in a less careful and rigorous study of God's word, because if we must avoid disputes and disagreements at all costs, what would be the point of a serious debate over what the Scriptures actually say.

Ultimately what we end up doing is diluting or polluting many of our most essential doctrines, all in the so-called name of Christian harmony. Harmony in the body of Christ is good, but never at the cost of a healthy inquiry into the true meaning of our Christian faith and heritage as God has revealed it in His Word. God's love ought to be able to lead us towards the truth not away from it.

Perhaps the most serious drawback to harmony at any price, is that what we believe about the nature and work of God, the nature and characteristics of our fallen humanity, and ultimately the central core of the Christian faith, which is the grace found only in our Lord Jesus Christ, are all placed in jeopardy. The constant erosion of the truths that constitute the main landmarks of Christianity and mark the path the Church should be following, results in a shallow, insipid faith. The faith we are left with comes nowhere close to resembling a mustard seed, nor is it capable of casting even a small stone into the sea, let alone a mountain.

From what we are seeing, the Church standing at the threshold of the Twenty First Century desperately needs to recapture the vibrant faith promised in the New Covenant and displayed in the First Century

Church. To do this we must begin back in the Garden of Eden, and what actually happened there. The all important question we need to resolve is what happened to you, me, and to everyone else in the world as a result of the fall of man. The question we need to answer first is this: Are the unsaved [which includes us] really dead, as God described it, or were we just wounded? Turning this question around, what we are asking and need to answer is how much of our salvation truthfully and practically depends on the working of our sovereign God, and how much of our salvation depends upon fallen man?

Depending on what we conclude from this debate, our answer will place either a greater or lesser emphasis on the consequences to us from original sin and the fall of man in Adam. This in turn will impact the power or lack of it in every Christian's life by determining how great our need is for the power of God's grace to work in us. If I was really dead [completely separated from the life of God], then I will believe that only the power of God and the resurrection of Christ can truly save me. On the other hand, if I conclude that my death is merely a metaphor for how seriously I was wounded, then I will more readily believe that God has power but it is limited by the choices I make.

Whatever the cause of our Biblical ignorance, instead of debating and arguing, perhaps we could better spend our time discovering what God says. For example, in Ephesians 2:1-10 God says, "And you were dead in your trespasses and sins, in which you formerly walked according to the course of this world, according to the prince of the power of the air, of the spirit that is now working in the sons of disobedience. Among them we too all formerly lived in the lusts of our flesh, indulging the desires of the flesh and of the mind, and were by nature children of wrath, even as the rest. But God, being rich in His mercy, because of His great love with which He loved us, even when we were dead in our transgressions, made us alive together with Christ (by grace you have been saved), and raised us up with Him, and seated us with Him in the heavenly places, in Christ Jesus, in order that in the ages to come He might show the surpassing riches of His grace in kindness toward us in Christ Jesus. For by grace you have been saved through faith; and that not of yourselves, it is the gift of God; not as the result of works, that no one should boast. For we are His workmanship, created in Christ Jesus for good works, which God prepared beforehand, that we should walk in them." Please observe that in verse 1 and again in verse 5, man is referred to as being *dead* because of his trespasses and sins.

Romans 6:23 says "...the wages of sin is death..." Romans 8:10-11 says, "And if Christ is in you, though the body is dead because of sin, yet the spirit is alive because of righteousness. But if the Spirit of Him who raised Jesus from the dead dwells in you, He who raised Christ Jesus from the dead will also give life to your mortal bodies through His Spirit who indwells you." I Corinthians 15:20-22 says, "But now Christ has been raised from the dead, the first fruits of those who are asleep. For since by a man came death, by a man also came the resurrection from the dead. For as in Adam all die, so also in Christ all shall be made alive." Colossians 2:13 says, "And when you were dead in your transgressions and the uncircumcision of your flesh, He made you alive..." Ephesians 2:1-10 also tells us that God made us alive while we were dead [verse 1]. God gave us the faith to believe as a gift [verse 8]. God created us for good works, which He has already prepared beforehand [verse 10]. Ephesians 1:3-14 repeatedly tells us what God has done, how He "has blessed us with every spiritual blessing ... in Christ." Salvation was never about what we must do, because only God can do these wonderful things to us and through us!

Philippians 1:6 says "...I am confident of this very thing, that He who began a good work in you will perfect it until the day of Christ Jesus." Again in Philippians 2:13 it says "...it is God who is at work in you, both to will and to work for His good pleasure." I Thessalonians 5:24 says "Faithful is He who calls you, and He also will bring it to pass."

The great beauty of grace is that it is all about what God has done, is doing, or will do, not about man having to perform this or achieve that in order to gain God's favor and approval. God accepts us because of what Christ has done, not because of what we do, whether good or bad!

When Romans 3:23 says we have sinned and fallen short of God's glory, does this mean we were just wounded by original sin and the fall? Or is God saying we are dead in our trespasses and our sins, and now our only hope of salvation is for Jesus to spiritually resurrect us from the dead?

How about it? Do you think we just need some first aid from a good Samaritan, or like Lazarus, do we need resurrection from the dead? As a result of the fall and original sin, are the unsaved just wounded, or are they dead? What about you; were you dead or were you just wounded? What do you believe? More *importantly*, what does the Bible say because this is what we all must believe. As it is written:

"And you were **dead** in your trespasses and sins"
Ephesians 2:1

Chapter Four

REDISCOVERING GOD'S PLAN
FOR SALVATION

(The Protestant Reformation)

BY GRACE THROUGH FAITH

The Christian faith has always been under attack and this will continue until our Lord returns. John 8:31-32 tells us that "...Jesus was saying to those Jews who had believed Him, 'If you continue in My word, then you are truly disciples of Mine; and you will know the truth, and the truth will make you free.'"

Four important things are revealed in this statement:

1) Jesus was *speaking to believers* [in this case Jews];
2) The true disciples of Jesus *will continue in His word* [be good students of the Bible];
3) These true believers will *understand God's truth* [able to apply God's truth];
4) *God's truth will set us free* [from guilt, fear of failing and wasted lives].

Satan's historical response to Christianity recognizes he can do nothing to stop the elect from believing. However, Satan also realizes he can counteract much of the benefits of our salvation and impact by keeping us Biblically *ignorant*.

We know Satan is a liar and the father of lies. He will continually try to deceive us by supplanting the truth with carefully constructed lies because this is his nature. His lies are carefully constructed with worldly 'wisdom' while maintaining a false religious appearance. A careful study of the Church's history and doctrinal teaching will clearly reveal this growing secular influence on true Christian doctrines and the damage that results.

Fortunately Satan's deceptions and distortions are periodically subjected to a fresh infusing of God's truth into His people to confront and counteract religious secularism. These are known as *revivals*. They can, however, take different forms and sometimes only affect certain cultures. The Great Awakening in 19th Century America is one such example. However, the 'mother' of all revivals so far was the Protestant Reformation begun in the 16th Century. The Reformation sought to rediscover the truth about salvation and to reform the Church concerning the significant difference between true faith and dead, useless works.

This world changing reformation began when a German monk, priest, and professor named Martin Luther wrote a ninety five point proposal for theological debate. It was written in Latin because the invitation to debate was intended only for other teachers and professors.

Luther was a professor at the University of Wittenberg in Germany, and the door of the Wittenberg Chapel was the University's bulletin board. The proposal, which is known as the Ninety Five Theses, was posted on the door of the Chapel on the eve of all saints, October 31, 1517. A German printer who understood Latin translated the Theses into German and published it. The rest is history.

Central to Luther's theses was God's plan of salvation and its abuse by the Church. One of the recurring violations of God's Word concerns the conditions God has set for salvation. It is the result of not understanding the critical differences between the Law and grace and between good works, works of the flesh and most importantly faith.

The inevitable result of not recognizing or understanding this critical difference is for the Church to succumb to religious secularism, teaching that salvation is a combination of belief and good works. Luther discovered the exceptional difference between Law and grace in Romans 1:17, which maintains that a person can only achieve a state of salvation and righteousness before God by faith alone.

Luther's goal in writing the Ninety Five Theses was to protect his flock and the Church from bad theology and its consequences. Each succeeding generation of Christians since 1517 has been passed the

Reformation's torch of spiritual enlightenment. Some have carried the torch well; others have stumbled and even let it go out.

THE EVOLUTION OF THE CHURCH

By the end of the first century, the Bible was completed. Those who try to maintain otherwise simply lack spiritual enlightenment themselves. Several house churches had been established but there were no church buildings. As the Church or body of Christ expanded more house churches were planted. The earliest known church building was a remodeled home in Philippi dating from the Second Century.

Larger cities soon had several congregations in them. To oversee and govern this expansion Bishops were being appointed in the major cities throughout the Roman Empire, leading to a ruling hierarchy. Naturally, Bishops needed large cathedrals and monks needed large monasteries. Along with church growth came new and different ideas and opinions about what the Scriptures actually teach. Trying to reinterpret Scripture to justify some human opinion or desire, unfortunately, seems to be a time honored tradition of Christianity

During the early centuries, various church councils were convened whenever serious disputes arose, usually theological in nature, which needed to be settled. From these debates, conclusions were reached which still aid our understanding of the Bible. For example, the issue of Christ's humanity versus His divinity was a point of contention until one of these councils resolved the problem by declaring that Jesus Christ was both 100% fully human and 100% fully divine.

During the second century, the Canon of Scripture was established, the Canon meaning the officially recognized [or authentic] books of the Bible. The consensus of most Christian groups then and now is that there are still the same sixty six books of both the Old and New Testaments.

Of course, there were many minor conflicts that also needed resolution, and in most cases advice was sought from the most respected of the Bishops. At that time everyone was accustomed to having civil disputes settled by the Emperor in Rome, and so the Bishop of Rome became the first among equals over the Church. From this pattern emerged the Papacy, although it was not called this until many centuries later in reaction to the Reformation.

During the middle Ages, the center of power of the Church moved back and forth between the bishop of Rome in the West and the bishop of Constantinople in the East. This ambivalence over the two centers of power finally led to the Great Schism in 1,000 A.D. The Eastern Orthodox Church, led by the Patriarch of Constantinople, expanded north and east, while the Western or Roman Catholic Church, led by the Pope in Rome, retained its power in central and southern Europe and across much of North Africa.

The Roman Catholic Church became very strong and powerful, sometimes vying with the State for control. The authority of the Roman Catholic Church was hierarchical [one human leader at the head] in structure, as was the Roman Empire. More and more, the Church adopted secular forms of organization and consequently, practice. More or less by default, the Pope became the 'emperor' of the Church and the final arbiter in Church matters. To this day, the Roman Catholic Church [i.e., the Pope], rather than the Scriptures, is the final authority over the doctrine and practice of the Roman Catholics.

Whenever a small group of people gains absolute control over something as large and as powerful as the Holy Roman Catholic Church, their primary goals will always be to remain in power and to retain their control. Consequently, every thing that is taught and every thing that is done will be focused on keeping these leaders in power and maintaining control. Although this goal is totally secular in nature, it still results in influencing both theology and practice.

One of the chief ways churches, including the Roman Catholic Church, try to maintain control is by promoting people's guilt and fear rather than relieving it. The Law is perfectly suited for this purpose; grace obviously is not. A crucifix which always portrays Christ suffering on the cross, and intercessory prayers to Mary because surely she would be more understanding and accessible than her angry Son whose crucifixion we helped cause, actually serve as continual reminders of our sin and guilt.

To a greater or lesser degree many churches, both Protestant and Catholic, use guilt and the fear of disappointment and punishment to maintain control and stay in power. Their motives may be sincere in their own eyes but biblically this is all horribly wrong. Until believers start immersing themselves in God's truth, bad doctrine will continue unchallenged, the Church will remain unchanged even though many in the Church bemoan the need for reformation, and Christians will continue to suffer from the lack of grace.

SIN, SACRIFICE, AND CONFESSION

The only source of comfort for guilty sinners in the Roman Catholic Church comes from making confession of their sins to the Church's priests. These priests alone have the power to forgive sin and determine whatever *penance* [or *works*] must be done to placate the wrath of God.

There are some grave problems that emerge when we think of *confession* as being a necessary requirement for our sins to be forgiven. Roman Catholic practice requires *confession* to a priest and *penance* as necessary steps to receiving God's forgiveness. Mainline Protestants and Evangelicals use confession in much the same way, except that they urge confession to God rather than to a priest or pastor. Nevertheless, either way, *confession* remains a condition or *requirement* for forgiveness.

We have here what should be easily recognized as a major doctrinal conflict, but for some reason it isn't. Catholics, Protestants, and Orthodox all correctly believe that according to Scripture there is only *one* sacrifice for sin, and only Jesus could make that necessary one-time sacrifice for sin on the cross at Calvary. Nevertheless we continue to insist that *confession* is necessary for forgiveness of our sin, and if we resist confession our sin remains unforgiven. This means we believe that unless we confess, God is not able to forgive our sins. Without realizing it, what we are doing is adding another sacrifice for sin besides the cross. This is a source of much confusion even today!

The problem really stems from two mistaken concepts about what confession is. One concept is that salvation is impossible without the sinner's conscious and intentional participation, which is confession. This makes confession a condition for forgiveness and without it God cannot forgive. This also makes confession a work of man and this certainly will not do. It also raises an interesting question, like what will happen if I forget and do not confess all of my sins?

This brings up the question of what confession is for and what it actually means. The word *confession* (*homologeo*) means to agree or admit to something. The word itself is a compound, *homo* meaning the same and *logo* meaning to speak or say. Confessing to God is simply saying the same thing as God meaning, "God you're right I am doing the wrong thing." If I confess Jesus as Lord it means I agree that Jesus as Lord. My belief or lack of it does not change Christ's lordship. If I confess a particular sin of which I have become convicted by the work of the Holy Spirit, I am admitting it is true and agreeing with the Spirit that I have indeed sinned. In other words, I stop lying to God, myself and others.

There is a critical difference for confessing our sins. Do we confess our sin in order to earn God's approval making confession a *cause*, or do we confess our sin as a result of God bringing something to our attention making confession a *response*? As a cause, confession becomes an additional requirement for sin to be forgiven, while as a response confession to God gives us insight and relief [See Psalms 32:3-5].

Agreeing with God and admitting the truth to Him does not mean He can't do something without my permission such as forgiving me. After all, He convicted me without asking my permission didn't He? By the same token, what would be the point of correcting or healing me without my first being made aware of my sin. The critical conflict we should be seeing and be deeply concerned about is that when we add conditions like confession to Christ's work on the cross than we deprive Christ's sacrifice and the cross of its truly singular importance and significance.

Obviously we are not to saying that confession has no place in the Christian life. We have already explained confession's role in dealing with the unnecessary burden of our guilt and in this case, confession [agreeing with God] is made on the basis of the finished work of the cross. Making confession to God an appropriate *response* to our sin and guilt is vastly different from making confession a condition or *requirement* for the forgiveness of sins. We must not confuse the purpose of confession with Christ's work of redemption and justification on the cross.

The other significant drawback to associating confession with being forgiven for our sins is the repetitiveness of confession. Every time we acknowledge or confess our sin to God, it is a reminder that we will be back, again and again, because our daily Christian lives will never be completely free of sin. This is fine as long as confession is associated in our thinking with sanctification, which is correct. However, if confession is connected to justification, then the reminder we are sending ourselves is that we will need to be repeatedly justified, which is false.

This is the same problem for those who are under God's Laws. The annual ritual sacrifices under the Old Covenant for the sins of the people, were never fully adequate either because they had to be repeated continually. And as Hebrews 10:3 says, "But in those sacrifices there is a reminder of sins year by year." The same holds true for confession if it is not correctly understood.

It was Lord Acton (1834-1902) who said, "Power tends to corrupt, and absolute power corrupts absolutely." Before the Protestant Reformation, Biblical interpretation was a closely guarded prerogative of the Church. The church maintained that ignorant peasants had no business investigating the Scriptures on their own [assuming they could even read]. Consequently, the church controlled what the Bible said allegedly to prevent misunderstanding, and even perverting what Scripture said.

Of course, this also left the church free to ignore, twist and even pervert the Bible's teachings with impunity. The general Biblical ignorance of the people was one of the big problems the Reformers were up against. In fact, Biblical ignorance is the main reason for having to instigate reform as well as the biggest obstacle to reform. Therefore, one of the main goals of the Reformers was to get the Bible into the hands of the people in their native tongue so they could read it and understand it for themselves. Need we say more?

Various attempts at reforming the church occurred over the years prior to the Protestant Reformation. However, they usually resulted in the reformers being burned at the stake for heresy. On October 31, 1517, the eve of All Saints Day when the church honored her martyrs, a German Augustinian monk named Martin Luther nailed something called the 95 Theses to the door of the Wittenberg Chapel. Thus began the Protestant Reformation.

THE REFORMER HIMSELF

Whenever the Church gets off course in its teaching and/or practice, God sets about getting it back on course. At no time was this more evident than in the Protestant Reformation. God chose a German

Dominican monk, priest, and professor of theology at the University of Wittenberg named Martin Luther (1483-1546) to ignite the Reformation.

During his monastic career, Luther suffered greatly with guilt, and frequently resorted to whipping himself on the back in an effort to punish himself for his sins and to relieve at least some of his guilt. Finally, the vicar-general of Luther's monastic order, Johann von Staupitz, advised Luther to lay aside the theological commentaries of the church and just study the Scriptures in the hope he might find some peace. Fortunately for Luther and for all of Christendom, he found it.

One day, while studying the Bible, Luther came upon Romans 1:16-17. It states; "For I am not ashamed of the gospel, for it is the power of God for salvation to every one who believes, to the Jew first and also to the Greek. For in it the righteousness of God is revealed from faith to faith; as it is written, 'But the righteous man shall live by faith.'"

Suddenly Luther got it. Because of the death of Christ on the cross, God had *already* forgiven Martin Luther. Because of Christ and His death, burial, and resurrection, Martin Luther already had the righteousness of Christ imputed to him. All Martin Luther had to do was believe this and receive it by faith, which God also enabled him to do!

God continued opening Luther's mind and heart to the truths of Scripture, and the more Martin continued to grow in grace, the more he realized that the Holy Catholic Church, which he served, had theologically gone off the track on several significant issues.

Luther loved the Lord and simply wanted to serve Him and His Church. Leading the greatest spiritual movement since the First Century was the furthest thing from Luther's mind. All he wanted to do was challenge other Catholic scholars and teachers to reconcile and return the Catholic Church to the truth and authority of God's word, the Bible.

However, as we all know, no good deed goes unpunished. For his efforts to reform the church [and it badly needed reforming], Luther was excommunicated. Nevertheless, the Protestant Reformation was underway and had the leader God chose.

GIVING BIRTH TO THE REFORMATION

Several events both near and far conspired to produce the Protestant Reformation. The emergence of the Renaissance period gave birth to a renewed interest in classical literature, knowledge, and the advanced cultures of the Greeks and Romans. This renewed interest in ancient literature included the Hebrew and Greek Scriptures. Also there was the invention of the printing press with movable type.

The building of St. Peters Basilica in Rome and the Pope's need to finance this project led to the sale of Papal Indulgences as a fundraising activity. The purchase of a Papal Indulgence granted the purchaser a shorter stay in purgatory and a quicker trip to the Pearly Gates. One could even purchase a deceased relatives freedom. The more one spent, the greater the benefit.

One particularly successful salesman of these Indulgences was a Dominican friar named Johann Tetzel. Tetzel's sales activities in a nearby community and his convincing sales pitch had drawn some of Luther's parishioners to buy these indulgences. Luther was infuriated over what he correctly considered a heretical desecration of the Biblical truth of salvation by grace through faith. The sale of Papal Indulgences became the last straw that resulted in Luther's debate challenge known as the Ninety Five Theses.

Be assured, the Protestant Reformation is the single most significant Christian event since the establishment of Christianity in the First Century! The actual event that sparked the Protestant Reformation was the work of an anonymous German printer in Wittenberg who also happened to read Latin. He saw Luther's 95 Theses [which was written in Latin] and concluded that this was some important stuff. So he translated Luther's Ninety Five Theses into German, printed them up on his new printing press and began distributing them.

The circulation of this document and the points it made about grace and faith soon began to cut into Johann Tetzel's profits, which is to say, it was cutting into the Pope's fund raising. The church ultimately responded by excommunicating Luther, and at one point, several nobles loyal to the Pope sought to kill Luther.

Some friends literally kidnapped Luther to protect him. They hid him for some ten months in the Wartburg Castle. While in seclusion at the Wartburg, Luther translated the entire New Testament into German in 11 weeks. Later, he also translated the Old Testament into German.[5] His work was so accurate that many German's still use Luther's translation today.

Although all believers are benefactors of the Reformation, the primary benefactors are those known as Protestants. Today there are more than three hundred Protestant denominations who can trace their origins back to Luther and the Reformation.

Although the Protestant Reformation *began* in 1517, it is still not completed. There is still so much in current theological belief and church practice that needs to be carefully re-examined and *reformed* in light of what the Scriptures actually teach! All Christians today are still part of the great Protestant Reformation.

THE NEXT REFORMATION

Over the years I have had the opportunity to visit a number of evangelical churches, and the one thing almost all have in common, is a central or core focus on evangelism. This is why they are called Evangelicals. The worship services, sermons, and programs are primarily aimed at converting the unsaved who they are hoping will visit their church services, hear the gospel, and come forward to accept the invitation to receive Christ.

On the other hand, Churches that do *not* focus on evangelism are more likely to focus on social issues and services. Although I admit I am making some pretty broad generalizations, this is where most of the mainline denominational churches can be found. It is fair to say that their general lack of aggressive evangelism leaves them on the outside of the evangelical movement.

The practices and doctrinal emphases of these two groups tend to be consistent with their focus. Many if not most mainline churches exhibit considerable concern for social justice and equality. Unfortunately, focusing on these kinds of concerns has also resulted in these churches turning a fairly blind eye to some very significant Biblical truths such as sin, damnation, and regeneration.

Their most consistent failure is in relying on political agendas that seem to share their concerns over social justice and equality rather than developing goals and strategies that are Biblically sound. Nevertheless, despite their doctrinal problems, some of these churches accomplish a great deal of good in providing relief to many of society's disenfranchised groups.

What seems to be missing on both sides of the ledger is an accurate Biblical *balance* between opposing the sins of social injustice and resolving the underlying cause of sins through conversion. The advocates of social justice are constantly straining at gnats while swallowing whole theological camels. One example is that in their enthusiasm to secure women's rights and freedom of choice, they completely ignore the moral dilemma of an unborn baby's God-given rights and freedoms.

Meanwhile, the Evangelicals are so concerned about morality and moral justice that they forget they are supposed to be evangelizing the very people their moral fervor is driving away. They really need to remember that while they are so busy condemning things like abortion and homosexuality, the only candidates for evangelization on this planet are sinners. This group will not only include those getting abortions and those who are gay, it will also include embezzlers, thieves, rapists, alcoholics, drug addicts, prostitutes and that nice couple who lives next door.

My concerns are mainly over what goes on in the evangelical churches, so my comments are somewhat limited to what I see affecting them. The evangelical's continual focus on missions and evangelism keeps them thinking about and setting goals around numbers and the costs involved in achieving their numerical goals, while unintentionally ignoring the plight of the poor, the sick, the imprisoned, the unwed mother, and the gay community.

One of our big problems in the Evangelical movement is that an Evangelical church's or pastor's *success* is measured by what a friend of mine calls "*numbers, nickels, and noise.*" How many are coming, how many are being saved, how many programs and how large a staff can we afford, how many missionaries do we support, and how much money are we raising to make all of this happen? Evangelicals believe in and are quick to defend their priorities, goals, and methods, justifying what they do by their passion for saving souls. What they don't seem to realize is that their constant focus has shaped their theology and doctrine, rather than having the Bible *shape* their theology and doctrine and letting the Bible *define* their focus and the methods they will use.

THE REFORMATION QUIZ

It is to be hoped that everyone has been paying close attention ever since beginning chapter one, because today we have a **test** to take. Actually, this 'test' is a demonstration of some of the major doctrinal problems the Reformers sought to resolve which still confuse a great many evangelicals today. For many of us, this will be an eye opening experience. It was for me the first time I took it, so to enjoy the greatest impact of this test, please, no cheating!!

There is ONE correct statement about JUSTIFICATION in each of the ten pairs of statements below. Some of the pairs of statements may seem to be saying the same thing. I assure you they are not. Many of the first time test takers also complain that this 'test' is way too picky. The objective of this test is to help each of us learn to carefully observe what God says in His word. So, please pick the one statement you think is correct in each pair by circling A or B:

1. A. God gives a man right standing with Him by accounting him innocent and just.

    B. God gives a man right standing with Him by making him into an innocent and just person.

2. A. God gives a man right standing with Him by placing Christ's goodness and virtue to his credit.

    B. God gives man a right standing with Him by putting Christ's goodness and virtue into his heart.

3. A. God accepts the believer because of the moral excellence found in Christ Jesus.

    B. God makes the believer acceptable by infusing Christ's moral excellence into his life.

4. A. If a sinner becomes born again and is transformed in character, he will receive right standing with God.

    B. If a sinner accepts right standing with God by faith, he will then experience transformation in character.

5. A. We receive right standing with God by faith.

    B. We receive right standing with God by faith, which has become active through love.

6. A. We receive right standing with God by Christ living out His life of obedience in us.

B. We receive right standing with God by accepting the fact that Christ obeyed the Law perfectly for us.

7. A. We receive right standing with God by following Christ's example in dependence upon His enabling grace.

B. We follow Christ's example in dependence upon His enabling grace because His life has given us right standing before God.

8. A. God first pronounces that we are good in His sight, and then gives us His Spirit to make us good.

B. God first gives us His Spirit to make us good, and then pronounces that we are good in His sight.

9. A. Christ's intercession gives us favor in the sight of God.

B. Christ's indwelling gives us favor in the sight of God.

10. A. By the power of the Holy Spirit living in us, we can fully satisfy the claims of the Ten Commandments.

B. By faith in the doing and dying of Christ, we can fully satisfy the claims of the Ten Commandments. (The correct answers are given in the endnotes of this chapter.[6])

The reason these questions may seem awfully picky is because Satan has put a tremendous amount of effort into blurring the lines between God's truth and the devil's lies and deceptions. If the incorrect answers of this test formed the basis of one's life, the problems this would cause will become more evident as time passes. Remember, it was failure to distinguish the truth that allowed for the sale of indulgences. Consequences can be *costly* and *misleading* in many ways!

THE FIVE PILLARS OF THE REFORMATION

The 'battle cry' of the reformers was contained in five Latin phrases, which considered together identify the central errors the Church *still* needs to correct. The differences over these five issues are so vitally important to a correct understanding of Christianity that they resulted in permanently splitting the Western church into Catholics and Protestants. We always need to speak the truth in love, but sometimes we have to fight for the truth as well. To believe error is to open the door to heresy and apostasy, and we *do not* want to go there! Here are the five Latin terms that are the pillars of the Reformation and need to be the battle cry of 21st Century believers.

1. SOLA SCRIPTURA: The Scriptures Alone are our authority.

Sola scriptura is the first pillar. Without this pillar, the other four pillars would have nothing to support them. This Latin phrase means "*only the Scriptures.*" I think it is fair to say that if we could get Christians to lay aside there doctrinal hobby horses, from praying to Mary to speaking in tongues to how the world as we know it will end,[7] and humbly submit our beliefs to a careful, thorough study of Scripture, we could avoid a lot of strife and division in the Church, which *is* the Body of Christ. This would also result in a much better witness to the world which, believe it or not, still keeps an eye on us. Nevertheless, sometimes the issues are so important that if we can not find agreement then we do have to part ways.

This particular issue was about whom or what constituted the *final authority* in the Church. One group said it was the Church, with the Papal Bulls, edicts, and traditions. They maintained that it was the duty of the Priesthood to interpret the Holy Scriptures for everyone else. They saw no need for the general masses to have their own Bibles to read and study. In fact, they argued that individual Bible study would only lead to confusion, heresy, and apostasy.

I have seen modern Protestant Evangelical churches try to prevent home Bible studies for much the same reason. For many churches, study of the Bible is okay *only* as long as the church knows [*controls*] what is taught and said.

The Protestant reformers steadfastly maintained that the final authority must be the Word of God. They believed it was vitally necessary for every Christian to be able to read and understand the Word of God. Beside the opposition of the Church to this, the matter was further complicated by the fact that the only available Bible was the Latin Vulgate. Latin was the language of the scholars, not the common man. This explains why Luther translated the Bible (initially the New Testament) into German, so that everyone could read it. With the Renaissance came Gutenberg who invented movable type and the printing press. This wonderful invention made the Bible more readily available and affordable, and was indispensable to the growth and spread of the Protestant Reformation. The first book ever printed was the Gutenberg Bible.

Yes, the Church did divide over this debate, and today there are both Catholics and Protestants. And there are true believers in both camps. So which group really won the debate?

The more important question is who is the final authority of truth in *your* life? Are your beliefs really based on the Bible, or are they actually based on what some significant person in your life, perhaps a parent, favorite pastor, teacher, or home Bible study leader, told you the Bible taught?

The fact that the church is constantly being swept by one 'spiritual' fad after another, proves that many of us are swept along by these fads just because we trust what others tell us is true, rather than discovering the truth for ourselves. If you want to know the truth for yourself, then you will have to read the Bible for yourself. Not Bible commentaries or devotional books, not even this book, but the Bible! Sure, commentaries can help our understanding as can this book, but they can never ever take the place of the Bible! Let's stay on the path of the Reformers, affirming the first great pillar of the Reformation; the authority of the Scriptures [*Sola Scriptura!*].

2. SOLUS CHRISTUS: Christ Alone is our Lord

The second pillar of the Protestant Reformation is *Christ only* or *Christ alone*. Christians will all agree *intellectually* with the doctrine that only Jesus Christ alone can save us. However, when it comes to the way we pursue our daily affairs and live out the Christian faith, we demonstrate that many of us have great difficulty in accepting the fact that *only Christ* can save us. The modern Evangelical movement must be careful to not reject by its practice and teaching the fact that *only Christ* can save us.

To the contrary, however, Christians are bombarded with exhortations to be held accountable, not by God, but by each other. In this environment, spiritual growth becomes a matter of having someone always looking over your shoulder to make sure you don't slip and to confront [and even tattle] if you do. This is nothing more than the most heinous secular practice of making others behave out of *fear* of exposure and ridicule.

How in the world can such a muddled state of affairs exist in Christianity? Because the Church and Christians still have to live in the world. How dare anyone accuse Christians of gross hypocrisy? First of all, because we will be hard pressed to find an Evangelical pastor or layman who would not agree that it is up to each individual to *accept* or *reject* Christ as their Savior. Secondly, almost all Evangelicals believe that both salvation and living a spiritual life is dependant upon us making the proper use of our *free will* and making the *right choices. Choosing* Christ as Savior and *choosing* to live for Christ in a Godly manner are fundamental applications in most sermons preached every Sunday!

Another fact that supports this strange division or dichotomy between what we *say* we believe and the beliefs we actually *practice* is the fact that we are raised in a secular world. Secularism believes *individualism* and *self-sufficiency* are highly desirable traits to be sought after and developed. Our pioneering forefathers were all rugged individualists, so these appeals to man's own will still make perfect sense to their way of thinking and way of life.

We have inherited this thinking and have applied it to and perpetuated it in our capitalistic, free market economy. One of every concerned parent's goals is to teach their children to become self-sufficient, that is, to be independent and responsible, able to get along on their own. This ability to survive and succeed on our own is believed to be absolutely necessary to our daily survival in a harsh and unforgiving world.

Self-sufficiency may seem to be an asset but in many significant ways, self-sufficiency is a tremendous liability to Christians and to their effective spiritual service. It is vitally important to know one's limitations, particularly our spiritual limitations, and be able to admit them and submit them and ourselves to God. Individualism, independence, and self-sufficiency have no place in God's way of doing things, mainly because God does not need help. We are the ones in need of help, and lots of it!

The only limitations on God's power and sovereignty are the ones we *create* in our own minds. Our imagined limitations of God's limitless power and sovereignty *seem* to produce inconsistent action and conflicting beliefs in us, but the truth is there simply are no actual limitations on the Sovereignty of God or on His unlimited power.

Real wisdom manifests itself in being able to sort Biblical truth from secular nonsense, and in how to make dependence on God our central strategy for survival in this alien and hostel world. If *only Christ* can save us, as the Bible and the reformers constantly maintain, then why is there any talk about our 'free-wills' and on our having to carefully make the right choices? Is this what the Scriptures really teach? Or does the Bible say, "For I am confident of this very thing, that He who began a good work in you [justification] will perfect it until the day of Christ Jesus [being sanctified until we are glorified]." (Philippians 1:6)

Does the Bible tell us to make a decision to choose Christ and be saved, or does it actually say we are to *believe* in Christ and to *confess* Him, and we will be saved? Romans 10:9-11 says, "...if you confess with your mouth Jesus as Lord, and believe in your heart that God raised Him from the dead, you shall be saved; for with the heart man believes, resulting in righteousness, and with the mouth he confesses, resulting in salvation. For the Scripture says, 'Whoever believes in Him will not be disappointed.'"

Three times "believe" is advocated and twice "confess with your mouth" meaning to agree with God verbally and publicly, but there is nothing about our having to choose and make Christ our Lord and Savior. This is not being unnecessarily picky; it is being accurate and true to what God says. Emphasizing *belief* instead of making *choices* makes a big difference in how we evangelize and in how we grow spiritually. Why? Because *belief* is an appeal to God and grace by faith, while *choosing* is an appeal to our emotions and self-effort.

Imputed Versus *Infused* Righteousness

If you encountered problems with the Reformation Test, which almost everyone does, it is probably because a very important *distinction* is missing in most of today's spiritual instruction. This issue is closely related to *Solus Christus,* and to whether salvation is a *joint effort* of man and God, or the *exclusive domain and work* of our Lord Jesus Christ.

The salvation of one's soul can be illustrated by comparison to a man who falls off a ship into the sea. The Biblical question is this; is *salvation* throwing out a life ring, which the drowning man has to grab hold of and hang on to, *OR* is *salvation* diving to the bottom of the ocean to retrieve his dead, drowned body, raise him up and bring him back to life?

The issue this raises is whether we just need some help, in which case we could grab the life ring and hold on ourselves, thus contributing to our salvation, or are we actually *dead*, in which case our drowned, dead body must be retrieved by Someone else who can also revive us.

So far in our little analogy, if understood correctly, our man overboard who drowned has been rescued from the bottom of the sea and brought back to life. He has been born again [regenerated, Titus 3:5]; he is a new creature or creation. Anyone who has been born again has been justified, which means they have been delivered from the *penalty* of sin.

At the same time our *drownee* was born-again and justified, he also had the righteousness of Christ *imputed* to him. The dictionary says *impute* means to attribute or "to regard a quality such as righteousness that applies to somebody as also applying to another person associated with him or her." In our scenario it means that the former drowning victim has now had the righteousness of Christ put to his account.

What has *not* happened yet is that our born again victim has been *made* righteous. To *make* a person righteous is to *infuse* them with righteousness. Turning again briefly to the dictionary, we find *infuse* means to "*fill somebody* or something *with a* strong emotion such as hatred, enthusiasm, or desire, to fix an emotion, belief, or *quality* in somebody else."[8]

Justification frees us from the *penalty* of sin. We will still sin, but the *penalty* for our sin has already been paid by Christ. One more thing happens at this point. The recently resurrected, formerly drowned person is *covered* with the cloak of Christ's righteousness. All who gaze upon him from the heavenly places will see only this cloak.

However, underneath the cloak is a wet, dirty, smelly, recently revived corpse. This is *imputed righteousness*. We are not changed, we are accounted or considered to have righteousness, but we are to know and remember that it is Christ's righteousness, not ours [His cloak not ours]. When we examine ourselves we should *not* expect to find a perfectly sterling character without fault nor should we be disappointed when we don't. At the moment of our justification we are not granted infused righteousness, only imputed righteousness. Sanctification is the ongoing process through the rest of our lives where the Holy Spirit is gradually conforming us to the image of Christ [Romans 8:29]. All of Christ's righteousness is *imputed* to us at the first moment of our salvation when we are fully justified. This determines our place before God, which correctly understood, is fully and completely accepted in His Beloved Son.

Christian growth is gradually acquiring [infused] some of Christ's righteousness. This has absolutely *nothing* to do with our right standing with God. But not knowing the difference between *imputed* and *infused* righteousness leads to all sorts of erroneous doctrines, and ties up a lot of Christians in Gordian knots of guilt and discouragement.

3. SOLA GRATIA: By Grace Alone

The Reformation started with affirming the Bible as the *only* authority for Christians. We might add it is the Bible in the hands of the Holy Spirit, not in the hands of man, dealing directly with our own inner convictions. Secondly, the Reformation affirmed that salvation and justification are accomplished by Christ alone. Salvation is not and never can be a joint effort between man and God.

Now we arrive at the third pillar of the Reformation, *sola gratia* or by *grace alone*. The chief concern of the reformers was over the matter of a person's justification. They wanted to take salvation out of the hands of the Church, and return it to the rightful owner, God. So when the reformers talked about grace, it was always in this context of salvation, that is, being justified by grace before God, and by grace being spared from His wrath.

Since 1517, justification by grace alone still attracts a lot of attacks. The less we know and understand about grace, the happier Satan is. Certainly, the secular mind is far more comfortable with performing for a reward than it is with the idea of being rewarded while failing to perform. How many voices inside and outside the Church, down through the ages, objected in one way or another to giving man a free ride to heaven. The unbelievable freedom that comes with grace alone is hard for any of us to wrap our minds around fully.

Perhaps because of this difficulty, the Reformation stopped short on it's declarations about grace alone. That is, they stopped at justification. Consequently they failed to point out that however one is justified; it necessarily follows that they would have to be sanctified in the same identical manner. This is absolutely true because there is only ONE plan for salvation. In other words, since both justification and sanctification [and glorification] are parts of the one and only salvation that God has provided, it must all work on the same principle. If you are justified by grace through faith, then you must also be sanctified by grace through faith. On the other hand, if our salvation is a combination of God's work and man's efforts, this means both our justification and our sanctification are based on our efforts and God's work. Recall the vitally important question of Chapter Three? Are we *dead* or are we *just wounded*? Perhaps you can see now why the correct conclusion is so crucially central to living the Christian life successfully. If we are justified by grace alone, then we can only be sanctified by grace alone!

The reformers had their hands full explaining and proving Scripturally that justification was by grace alone. They succeeded remarkably when it comes to being saved or justified. But if you listen carefully to contemporary sermons, you will discover that while it is fine to be saved [i.e. justified] by grace alone, the messages on daily Christian living and growth depend on your efforts, and choices. Whereas you can't be saved [justified] by works, neither can you be sanctified without grace. This is an absurd impossibility that is constantly being taught in today's churches. Therefore, I believe it is imperative for us to complete the Reformation by exploring, defining, explaining, and learning to enjoy *sanctification* by grace alone.

4. SOLA FIDE: By Faith Alone

Sola fide means by faith alone. No one can be saved by works of the flesh or by keeping the Law. We can only be saved by grace alone working through faith alone. Not only is grace the free gift of God, so is *faith*. Ephesians 2:8-9 clearly states, "For by grace you have been saved through faith; and that not of yourselves, it is the gift of God; not as a result of works, that no one should boast."

If man must generate the faith to accompany grace for his salvation, then it has again become a joint effort by man and God. If God supplies us faith along with and as part of His grace, then salvation remains a work of Christ alone. And don't forget, if justification is by grace alone through faith alone, by Christ alone, according to the Scriptures alone, then so is our *sanctification*. Paul says in Galatians 2:20, "I have been crucified with Christ; and it is no longer I who live, but Christ lives in me; and the life which I now live in the flesh I live by faith in the Son of God, who loved me, and delivered Himself up for me."

Nevertheless, at the end of every sermon, an invitation is given, and the audience is urged to make a decision to come forward and choose to receive Christ as their Lord and Savior. Often audiences in church services are also warned not to reject Christ because that is choosing to go to Hell.

Did you know that the *invitation* to receive Christ normally given at the end of many Evangelical church services did not even exist until the 1800's when it was introduced by an evangelist named Charles G. Finney. To listen to some extol the importance of giving an invitation at every opportunity makes one wonder how anyone ever got saved before 1800.

Finney is considered a 'founding father' of the modern evangelical movement. Yet this man believed in no uncertain terms that there was no fall of man and no such thing as original sin. He viciously attacked the doctrine of Christ's substitutionary atonement [meaning Christ died in our place to pay our penalty for our sin], and Finney also completely repudiated the doctrine of justification by faith alone and the imputation of Christ's righteousness to a sinner by grace through faith. Why? Because his basic thesis was, that man had the necessary capacity to become righteous through his own choices and efforts.

Dr. R. C. Sproul, a member of the Alliance of Confessing Evangelicals and Chairman of Ligonier ministries in Orlando, Florida had this to say about C. G. Finney: "Now, if Luther was correct in saying that *sola fide* is the article upon which the Church stands or falls, if what the reformers were saying is that justification by faith alone is an essential truth of

Christianity, who also argued that the substitutionary atonement is an essential truth of Christianity, the only conclusion we can come to is that Charles Finney was not a Christian. I read his writings and I say, 'I don't see how any Christian person could write this.' And yet, he is in the Hall of Fame of Evangelical Christianity in America."[9] There is something to think about.

As to what the Scripture says about sanctification by grace alone through faith alone consider Paul's words in Galatians 3:1-3. "You foolish Galatians, who has bewitched you, before whose eyes Jesus Christ was publicly portrayed as crucified? This is the only thing I want to find out: Did you receive the Spirit by the works of the Law, or by hearing with faith? Are you so foolish? Having begun by the Spirit, are you now being perfected by the flesh?" The word "walk" in Scripture always refers to our daily sanctification experience, so when II Corinthians 5:7 says "...for we walk by faith, not by sight..." it is also telling us our sanctification is by faith alone. As with our justification, sanctification is never by works, but boy that's hard to remember!

5. SOLA DEO GLORIA: The glory and the praise is To God Alone

The fifth and final pillar of the Reformation was *sola Deo Gloria*, meaning for God's glory alone. The true heart of this statement has to do with whether we actually believe God is able to stand alone at the center of the universe and run it all by Himself. In other words, do we really believe God is sovereign? If God really is sovereign, then He is fully in charge, not only of the entire universe, but also of our lives. If only God alone can save us, and only God alone can sanctify us, and glorify us, then surely He alone is worthy of glory, and of our praise and worship. If our God is fully sovereign, and He certainly is, then what else is there to devote one's life to? We are supposed to live for God's will in all things. But do we or more to the point, why don't we?

Well sure, every Christian is going to say, "Of course, God is the center of the universe, this is absolutely true. God is sovereign. Everyone should glorify God." The problem is we do not *live* this way! The easiest way to check what I am suggesting is indeed true is for each of us to carefully and honestly examine our prayers. How *often* do we pray, *what* do we pray for, and *how* do we ask for it? Our answers should tell us whether we really do believe God is sovereign.

For example, do we treat God in our prayers as if He is just a heavenly bellboy, expected to humbly jump to meet our every request? You may say no way, but how do you react when God does *not* give you what you ask for? When God says *no*, are our concerns still for God's glory alone, or do we get all hurt and angry and start pouting? If we do, then we are obviously harboring and pushing a personal agenda *other* than Gods.

How many of us buy into the "name it and claim it" brand of Christianity; how do we pray, and what do we expect in return? What this seems to boil down to is a list of things God has promised to do or provide for everyone of us, and since we have a divine given right to these things, all we need to do is claim each of these items by 'faith' and they are ours.

I have noticed that within such groups, good health and financial success are two of the *big* things promised to all who have *enough* *faith*. To lack these things is to reveal one's lack of faith and spirituality. Miracle healing services are a regular feature in these groups.

This is really just a variation of the Holy Bellboy approach to God, with a menu to order from. But I bet you have never seen a 'name it and claim it' list that includes things like suffering, poverty, rejection, mourning, homelessness, humility, patience, self-control, disease, blindness, crippled limbs, false accusations, imprisonment, persecution, being crucified either upside down or right side up, beheaded, hung, burned at the stake, or any other form of martyrdom.

In fact, the only place I have ever seen such a list is here in the Bible, and this is the short list. All we have to do is recall some of the things that happened to our Lord, to His Apostles, and to His prophets. Jesus did say the disciple is not greater than his Lord, and that any who would follow after Him would also get to help fill up [complete] His sufferings. Nevertheless, Lord grant us the faith and the intestinal fortitude to conclude our prayers with a genuine, sincere, "not my will but thine be done!"

How can we pray for God's glory alone? Actually, any honest, sincere prayer is in and of itself a recognition and declaration that God alone is Sovereign, and that we are truly helpless. Just the fact I am praying is proof of my helplessness, and that I believe only God can do what is right and what is needed. And let us never forget that we exist Sola Deo Gloria, that is, Lord we exist for Your sake and glory alone. Amen!

MOVING ON

In Luke 6:46-49 Jesus said, "And why do you call Me, 'Lord, Lord,' and do not do what I say? Everyone who comes to Me, and hears My words, and acts upon them, I will show you whom you are like: "He is like a man building a house, who dug deep and laid a foundation upon the rock; and when a flood arose, the river burst against that house and could not shake it, because it had been well built. But the one who has heard, and has not acted accordingly, is like a man who built a house upon the ground without any foundation; and the river burst against it and immediately it collapsed, and the ruin of that house was great."

Jesus warned us about the kind of foundation we build our beliefs and lives on. In this first volume, Basic Grace, we have been concentrating on the doctrine of justification. We have been laying the only foundation upon which we can build Christianity.

The Reformation was all about reestablishing the truth that we are saved by grace through faith, not by Laws and works of the flesh. The foundation of grace and faith is justification. If we do not teach every new Christian the truth, the whole truth, and nothing but the truth about how we have come to be justified by God's grace through faith alone and what it really means, then they will not be prepared to weather life's many and often violent storms.

On the foundation for grace we have also seen five essential pillars erected. The first one is the Scriptures, and only the Scriptures. We must be Biblically literate because our first priority must always be, "... but what does God say?" The second pillar is Christ only. Others can provide assistance and input, but never in place of whatever will bring everyone's focus back on Christ, the only author and finisher of our faith. The third or middle pillar is grace, and only grace. We can only be justified by grace and we can only be sanctified by grace. The fourth pillar is by faith only. We cannot and must not try to mix Law with grace or works with faith. You will have much better luck mixing oil and water. The fifth pillar is that everything we think, say, and do should be for God's glory alone.

We can only accomplish these things if we are being led by Christ according to the Scriptures by grace through faith.

Chapter Five
THE BEST LAID PLANS ARE GOD'S

SAVING THE HUMAN RACE

God's plan of salvation is based exclusively on grace through faith. It always has been, it is now, and it always will be. God's plan of salvation has never been based on keeping the Law because we humans are incapable of keeping the Law. The purpose of the Law is to reveal our weakness and need for salvation and then lead us to Christ. This is God's best and only plan for our salvation.

By now you should be convinced that the Scriptures teach that the human race was not just wounded by sin, but that sin has *fatally* wounded us. Original sin and the fall left us *dead* in our sins and trespasses, and that is bad news. However, the good news is God has a plan for saving the human race, or at least a portion of it.

So far, we know two things for sure. One, we know we need to be saved, and two, we also know that it will take a lot more than band-aids and iodine to save us. As a matter of fact, since we are dead, it is going to take nothing less than the death and resurrection of Christ Jesus, God's own unique Son, to accomplish our salvation.

The reason for the time we spent in those first chapters was to establish both the *seriousness* and the *extent* of humanity's fall from innocence into sin and death. Through Adam and Eve, Satan has made sure that we have been dumped into the good old 'you know what' *without* a paddle. If you are as convinced as I am that our situation is desperate enough for us to need outside help, the good news is that God does have a paddle, and in fact, He has the *only* paddle. God does have a plan to rescue us, and it is the *only plan* that will work.

HISSTORY

It is said that the word *history* should really be spelled with a double "s." That would make it *His story*, which is what history really is. The reason for calling history *His story* is that God has been making Himself known to humanity ever since the beginning of time. Romans 1:18-20 says, "For the wrath of God is revealed from heaven against all ungodliness and unrighteousness of men, who suppress the truth in unrighteousness, because that which is known about God is evident within them; for God made it evident to them. For since the creation of the world His invisible attributes, His eternal power and divine nature, have been clearly seen, being understood through what has been made, so that they are <u>without excuse</u>." Psalm 96:4-5 says, "For great is the Lord, and greatly to be praised; He is to be feared above all gods. For all the gods of the peoples are idols [or *non-existent things*], but the Lord made the heavens." And Psalm 97:6 says, "The heavens declare His righteousness, and all the peoples have seen His glory."

Variations of this theme are repeated over and over in the Old Testament. The New Testament explains the plan and provides us with the 'paddle.' Throughout history, God has been teaching humanity about His plan for our salvation. The shedding of blood for the remission of sins plays a dominant role in the whole Jewish system of worship, always pointing forward to the day of Christ and the completion of our salvation at the cross in Christ.

The created world serves as a stage for demonstrating God's *righteousness* to all beings, heavenly and earthly. God's *righteousness* refers to His perfect moral purity, His absolutely fair and unbiased justice, and His limitless grace and mercy. It is also upon this stage that God will publically and completely defeat sin and Satan for all eternity. The next time anyone asks you about the meaning of life, well *now you know it!*

We humans do not exist as some sort of random cosmic accident, nor are we the result of an idle divine experiment. Contrary to popular or at least hopeful belief, we are not here to freely amuse ourselves any way we please, only to pass on into oblivion without any consequences. We *do* exist only because of God's plan and God's purpose. Starting with the Garden of Eden, through the world wide flood, to the creation of the nation of Israel and God's dealings with His Jews, especially in the giving of His Laws and commandments, to the cross with the resurrection and the ascension of Christ, to the rapture of the Church and the final seven years of tribulation, God is continually being *seen* and *heard* and *understood*. From the very beginning of time and history as we know it, God began revealing His perfect plan for *redeeming* us [literally buying back] and *saving* us from judgment, condemnation, and damnation!

This first hint of God's plan for saving us comes right after Adam and Eve commit the Original Sin by eating the forbidden fruit of the tree of the knowledge of good and evil. Suddenly realizing they are naked and that this is somehow wrong, they quickly sew for themselves loin coverings made from the leaves of a fig tree. Then when they hear God walking through the Garden, they hide from Him. Why? Because whether you are Adam and Eve, or Jim and Sally, our sin will always produce *guilt*, *shame*, and the *fear* of God's punishment. The natural reaction of every human being ever born is either to try to cover up and hide their sin, or to try to hide from God because they sinned, or *both*.

Sin not only produces guilt, shame, and fear of punishment, sin ALWAYS has *consequences*. Fortunately, in the case of Believers, because of the cross, the consequences are only temporal, never eternal. For example, Adam now had to labor hard for his 'daily bread' for the rest of his earthly life, as will every one of his male descendants. Eve will have pain in childbirth, as will every one of her female descendents! Additionally, Adam and Eve were permanently booted out of Paradise and there is no going back. Whether you are a Christian or not, don't ever expect to find a paradise here on earth. It is gone for good! [Genesis 3:14-24]

It is also true that God *always* has a plan for dealing with our sin. For example, in Genesis 3:21 we are told that God made garments of skin to replace Adam and Eve's fig leaf covering. In fact, the meaning of "covering someone's nakedness" in the Bible always refers to forgiving sins. It is also important to recognize that in order for there to be an animal skin, an animal had to be killed. In other words, it always takes a *blood sacrifice* to forgive our sins.

God sent His only Son, Jesus, to live here on Earth at a specific time in history. God also sent Him to accomplish a very specific mission. That very specific mission was to once and for all time effect our complete and eternal salvation on the Cross at Calvary. Jesus *is* the final, ultimate, and complete blood sacrifice for our sins. [See Galatians 4:4-7; Ephesians 1:10; Hebrews 9:11-15].

GOD'S PERFECT PLAN FOR SALVATION

We are now at that time in '*His Story*' known as the age of *grace*, or the Church age. It began with the cross and the resurrection of Jesus, and it will continue until the rapture of the church. This also means we are now under the New Covenant of Grace. The age of the Law and the Old Covenant ends and the age of Grace began with the death, burial, resurrection and ascension of our Lord Jesus Christ.

Now please take careful note of the following, and let me warn you in advance, you are going to hear a lot about it throughout this book. You will also hear a lot about it in the Bible. It is this: **No one has ever been saved by keeping the Law and no one ever will**! No one *except Jesus* has ever kept the whole Law.

There were people who were saved during the historical period when the Old Covenant of Law was in force, but salvation has always and only been by grace through faith. Noah, Abraham, Isaac, Jacob, Moses, David, and many others were saved by God, but always by grace through faith, never by works of the Law. Notice if you will, Romans 4:7-8, which is a quotation of King David from Psalm 32:1-2: "Blessed are those whose lawless deeds have been forgiven, and whose sins have been covered. Blessed is the man whose sin the Lord will not take into account." Those who were saved or are being saved, or ever will be saved, are saved only because they *believed* what God said. [Also, please see Hebrews 11:1-40]

We must never forget that God's perfect plan of salvation has *always existed* and has *never changed! It is Plan A. There is no Plan B.* We are told in Ephesians 1:3-4 that before creation, God chose us in Christ, "that we should be holy and blameless before Him." The only way anyone can be *holy* and *blameless* before God is if God *saves* that person by "*grace through faith*" and then *declares* that person to be righteous. [Ephesians 1:3-14; 2:8-9] No one has ever been saved or ever will be saved by the works of the Law, because they would have to be perfect to do it! And that would mean that God would have to move over because now there would be two of you.

It is also helpful to realize *why* God saves us. Ephesians 2:10 clearly states "For we are His workmanship, created in Christ Jesus for good works, which God prepared beforehand, that we should walk in them." The reason God saves us has *nothing* to do with whether we are good or bad people. God saves us, from the greatest to the least of us, not because we deserve saving, but because He has already chosen us and determined a specific purpose for us even before He created the world. [See Matthew 13:24-30, 36-43; and John 10:10b-11, 14-17]

Every Christian exists because God created us and then saved us for some specific purpose, which He alone has determined. Our weaknesses, disabilities, physical and emotional scars, sexual orientation, failures, habits, sins, inabilities, lack of knowledge, loss of health, immobility, age, yes the list is almost endless. What you are or are not has *everything* to do with God's intentions for you and *absolutely nothing* to do with whether or not you, or anyone else, thinks you are good enough or sufficiently worthy enough to be saved. No one but God has the right to judge a persons worth. Only God alone can declare a person worthy. Only God can choose to save us.

If you have any doubts about what I am saying, and most of us do at some point or other, then you **must** read Psalms 139:1-24 and I Corinthians 1:18-31, and I recommend you do so with a hi-lighting pen in hand. Please do not be afraid to hi-light passages of Scripture that speak to your heart or to make notes in the margins of your Bible. The Bible is the most important book you will ever own, so read it, study it, know it, apply it, and oh yes, mark it.

AS SIMPLE AS ONE, TWO, THREE

God's plan of salvation consists of *three* distinct phases. These stages or phases are *justification, sanctification,* and *glorification.* These three stages or phases always occur in that order, and they always work equally for everyone who is being saved. All three of these stages or phases always operate on the same basis, which Ephesians 2:8-9 tells us is by grace through faith, and that both grace and faith are a *gift* from God.

Justification, sanctification, and *glorification* may sound like some dusty old theological words, but they are, in fact, vital and literal Biblical words. *Justification, sanctification,* and *glorification* have very important and specific meanings, which *every* Christian really needs to understand accurately. Never forget that our common enemy, the devil, delights in messing us up every time he gets the opportunity. Using our ignorance or confusion over what *justification, sanctification,* and *glorification* actually mean and what they apply to always gives Satan a golden opportunity to truly foul up a Christian's life. Consequently please pay close attention to what follows!

PHASE ONE: WE ARE JUSTIFIED

Each of the three phases or segments of our salvation refers to our deliverance from a specific consequence of sin. The first phase of our salvation, *justification*, refers to God delivering us from the **PENALTY** of sin. You will recall passages we have noted, such as Romans 3:23 and 6:23, and Ephesians 2:1-10, which clearly teach that we are *dead* in our sins. This means that we are completely separated from God by our sins. Nothing could be more serious because we also know that the *penalty* for sin is **DEATH**. This means that without God's intervention on our behalf through Christ Jesus and the cross, we will remain eternally separated [dead] from God.

If this sounds like a sentence being handed down by the judge in a court of law, this is precisely what it is. All of us have broken one or more of the Ten Commandments at some time and probably most of them many times. This means we are *guilty* of breaking God's Laws and because of our crime; we have been sentenced to death, just as we were warned would happen.

God's court of justice is the Supreme Court for all Creation, there is *no higher court.* If you want to appeal His decision, the *only* appeal that God will allow is to the substitutionary death of Christ in our place. This is the undeserved but just and complete payment for our sins. If God had not sent His only unique Son Jesus to die on our behalf, our 'goose' would have been thoroughly and righteously cooked.

God has intervened on our behalf, not because He has to, but because He chose to and has always planned to. Our *deliverance* from the *penalty* of sin occurs because Jesus Christ went to the cross and died in our place. Our sin is not dismissed because God, the Lawgiver and Judge, is a really nice guy who loves us. No, our sin is forgiven because the full penalty for our sin was paid by the Lord Jesus Christ. It is the Judge's only Son who has been executed in our place!

Perhaps you have heard someone explain *justification* to mean "*just as if* I'd never sinned." Easy to remember, but it misses the point that I *did* sin, I *do* sin and I *will* continue to sin. This is the unvarnished truth and why Jesus had to die in my place so that I could be forgiven and set free. This is no hypothetical fairy tale; this is *ultimate reality*!

Each one is *justified* when Christ's death and burial is applied to them personally. *Justification* occurs *once* in each Christian's life, because justification is only *needed* once! *Justification,* meaning deliverance from the penalty of sin, occurs at the moment an individual understands, believes and confesses that Jesus Christ paid for all of that person's sins. Now he or she can know that not only are all their sins [past, present & future] forgiven, but they have also been declared [reckoned, considered] to be *righteous*.

DECLARED RIGHTEOUS

To be declared *righteous* is to have the *righteousness* of Christ put on your 'account.' It is a little like having someone else who is rich beyond measure put their money into your checking account. A person who is truly righteous before God is someone who is *always* morally upright, fair, just, compassionate and merciful. The only person in history to fit this description is Jesus Christ. Therefore, to be declared righteous by God means you literally have the righteousness of Christ put into your 'account' so that you can draw upon it whenever needed.

Being *declared righteous* occurs at the same moment we are *justified* and is an indispensable part of our *justification*. Now we need to be very careful not to make the same mistake others have made in the past on this matter. The critical fact is that we are not made righteous, but rather we are declared or considered or *reckoned* to be righteous, and therefore to be treated by God as someone who has the same quality of *righteousness* as our Lord Jesus Christ. We will *never* become fully righteous in this life, even though the process of *sanctification* will certainly improve our morality, our unbigoted and unbiased fairness, and our capacity for mercy and compassion. However, regardless of the actual level of our *righteousness*, God will always *consider* us to be as completely righteous as Christ because we are in Christ.

Because I have been *declared* [not made] righteous, God will never be my Judge again. Did you get that? God will *never* judge or punish anyone who is in Christ. What is even more amazing is the fact because we are reckoned as righteous God has also adopted us into His family. Now God is my Father, forever. Talk about not getting anything you do deserve, and instead getting everything you want, need, and know you *don't* deserve. Grace may be a free gift to you and me, but it is not a cheap gift. It is the most valuable gift any human being could receive, and therefore, grace must never be ignored or trivialized in our teaching.

Since we did nothing to earn or deserve salvation in the first place, no matter what phase of salvation we are in, be it *justification, sanctification*, or *glorification*, we can also do nothing to lessen or cause the loss of our salvation. Grace is the most wonderful, most precious, most expensive, and most necessary gift any one has ever received! And it will never wear out or be out of style!

While our experiences will differ during the sanctification process, we all share one fact that is the same for all believers. We are all born in sin, and we have all broken God's commandments repeatedly, proving we are sinners. We know we are sinners and we know we need to be forgiven. We know only God can do this and we have gratefully trusted Him to do just that, *forgive* us. Having been forgiven, we also understand that we have been justified. This means we are no longer sinners. In fact we are, along with every other Christian, a **saint** [I Corinthians 1:1 2], ready to begin the process of sanctification.

THE CERTIFICATE OF DEBT

There is a powerful passage in Colossians that not only states in no uncertain terms the impact justification has on us, it also contains a remarkable illustration of our justification. Colossians 2:13-14 says, "And when you were dead in your transgressions and the uncircumcision of your flesh, He made you alive together with Him, having forgiven us all our transgressions, having cancelled out the Certificate of Debt consisting of decrees against us and which was hostile to us; and He has taken it out of the way, having nailed it to the cross."

At the heart of this passage is the reference to a "Certificate of Debt" which contains decrees against us, and which ends up being cancelled out by being nailed to the cross. This illustration explains what happened to our sins when Christ Jesus was crucified in our place. This illustration is also set in the first century world, using terminology and practices familiar to the original audience.

The key word in this illustration is *cheirographon*. This Greek word literally means *handwriting*, however its use here and throughout the First Century world was as a legal technical term. This word, cheirographon, is only used once in the Bible. It is the title of a legal document, accurately translated as the Certificate of Debt. It was a hand written and signed document made out by anyone who borrowed money, or otherwise incurred a financial obligation. This document was then held by the one to whom the money was owed, until the debt was paid in full. In today's terminology it might be called a *promissory note*, a *contract* of some sort, or a *mortgage*. If you signed a Certificate of Debt, it meant you owed a certain amount of money to the holder of that certificate and you were obligated to pay it back in full.

The use of a Certificate of Debt was expanded under the Roman legal system. It came to be used not only for a person's financial debts, but also for their *social* debts. It became the written record of a convicted felon's *debt to society*. The Certificate of Debt was written up by the court stating the crimes the felon has been convicted of, and the sentence he is to receive. The Certificate of Debt was then *nailed* to the felon's prison door. Anyone who cared to read the Certificate of Debt would know *who* was in that prison cell, *why* they were there, and for *how long*! This Certificate was obviously hostile to the felon or the debtor, until the sentence was completed or the money was fully repaid.

When the debt was finally paid, something very interesting happened. The Certificate of Debt was taken by a prison official or the holder of a monetary debt and they would write across the Certificate of Debt the Greek word *tetelestai*. This Greek word meant the same thing as our stamping a bill or receipt *"PAID IN FULL."* [10]   The Certificate of Debt was then given to the former debtor or prisoner, giving him proof he had fully paid his debt, whatever it was, and could never be held responsible for that debt again.

The significance of this to us is found in John 19 where the crucifixion of our Lord is recorded. In verse thirty, the last thing Jesus did before giving up His spirit was to utter a phrase in Aramaic, the language common to Jews at this time. The inspired record, the Bible, is written in Greek, so whatever Jesus said was translated into Greek. Our Lord's final statement from the cross was *"It is finished."* That's what it says in our English translations, like the New American Standard Bible. What the Greek text says, by the inspiration of the Holy Spirit, is that our Lord's final word was *"tetelestai,"* meaning the debt has been **PAID IN FULL!**

There is more! In the instance of a capital crime where the defendant was found guilty and sentenced to death, his Certificate of Debt accompanied him to the place of his execution. For the Romans, execution would be by crucifixion. The Certificate of Debt was nailed to the cross over the defendant's head, so that any onlookers could see exactly who was up there, and why he was being executed.

At the insistence of the Jewish leaders, Pontius Pilate, the Roman governor, finally ordered Jesus to be crucified. Pilate also specified what would be said on our Lord's Certificate of Debt. By Pilate's order it read *"JESUS THE NAZARENE, THE KING OF THE JEWS"* in three languages.

Now look at the rest of Colossians 2:13-15, which constitutes the immediate context of the Certificate of Debt. The precision of the Greek language will always add to our appreciation and understanding of God's Word. [11]

"AND WHEN YOU WERE DEAD..." the word dead here meaning a dead body or corpse, and the verb here is a Greek present tense, referring to a continuous state. This makes the obvious meaning of *dead* even more obvious, for if someone is dead, then they are hopelessly lost. After all, what can a corpse do besides rot?

"IN YOUR TRANSGRESSIONS AND THE UNCIRCUMCISION OF YOUR FLESH..." This next phrase begins with *"in"* meaning *"by reason of"* and describes in general what is universally true of all who are spiritually dead. We are dead because of our "transgressions" and "uncircumcision." "Transgressions" means to trespass, or to *intentionally* do what we shouldn't do or go where we shouldn't go and don't belong. The "uncircumcision of your flesh," is a colorful way of describing anyone who is outside the faith. The figurative meaning of "flesh" refers to our natural, human, material self, as opposed to our spiritual self. So far, we have a concise and accurate description of a person without Christ. Another point that must not escape our attention is the fact that we are also as helpless as a corpse!

"HE MADE YOU ALIVE TOGETHER WITH HIM..." This phrase contains the main verb in this portion of the passage. It is *"made you alive"* which is an aorist verb, meaning it was a specific action taken at some point in time, and not some ongoing or conditional process. The only way we can overcome spiritual death is when God alone makes us alive, and He does this by identifying us as eternally being "with him," our Lord Jesus, in His death, burial, and resurrection.

How God makes us alive is described by two aorist participles, which modify the main verb. The first participle is *"having forgiven us..."* The grammatical construction here also indicates that to make us alive, God first has to forgive us *"all our transgressions."* The word *"forgiven"* has in its root meaning the word *charis*, or *grace*. Again, *"transgressions"* means trespasses, or willful sins.

"HAVING CANCELLED OUT..." This phrase, the other aorist participle, not only modifies the main verb, it also precedes "FORGIVEN," giving us the sequence of how forgiveness takes place. Christ's death on the cross first "cancelled out the Certificate of Debt" which each of us unfortunately possesses. Each of our individual and personal Certificates of Debt is made up of "decrees against us." Like every other criminal's Certificate of Debt, our every violation of the Law is recorded here. And the sentence for our violations is death [Romans 6:23]! But once our debt is paid, it removes us from a legal relationship with God as our Judge. Now God has a perfectly legitimate and legal basis upon which to graciously forgive us, make us alive and adopt us into His family, all through His Son Jesus.

When Christ Jesus was nailed to the cross, He was taking our place, and each of our Certificates of Debt were nailed there over His head. The crowds only saw a Certificate of Debt that said "Jesus the Nazarene,

King of the Jews"[12], but God saw each of our own personal Certificates of Debt nailed there. And it is all of these debts that Jesus *Paid In Full*!

Hopefully, the full impact of this passage will grip us in the same fashion it did any first century citizen. Because Jesus died in my place, my Certificate of Debt now has *tetelestai* written right across the middle of it. If you are a born-again believer, you have a Certificate of Debt too, with *tetelestai* written boldly across it! Our debt has been fully paid by our Savior, so we can never be legally charged with our sins again! This is what it means to be *justified!*

PHASE TWO: WE ARE BEING SANCTIFIED

The second phase of our salvation is *sanctification*. *Sanctification* is about God *progressively delivering* us from the **POWER** of sin. By definition, to *sanctify* something or someone means to *be set apart and put to its intended purpose or proper use*. For example, when you comb your hair, you are sanctifying your comb by putting it to its intended use. And when you put it back in your pocket or purse, you are setting it apart to use again for its intended purpose.

In *salvation*, our *sanctification* means we are being set apart by and for God, and being put to the use for which God created us. Since we were always destined for God's exclusive use, we now have, at least in broad terms, the *WHY* of why we are here.

This does not mean we all have the exact same purpose or mission in life. We are taught in Romans 12:3-8, I Corinthians 12:1-31, and Ephesians 4:1-16, that we Christians are all part of one spiritual body, the universal body of Christ, or the Church. And just like a human body with arms and legs, our spiritual gifts and jobs are different.

BECOMING LION FOOD

I Peter 5:8 says "Be of sober spirit, be on the alert. Your adversary, the devil, prowls about like a roaring lion, seeking someone to devour." One of the ways the devil gets to take a serious bite out of us is when we confuse what *justification* **is** with what *sanctification* **does**. Anytime we base our beliefs and decisions on feelings or other's opinions, rather than on Biblical truth, we become extremely vulnerable to Satan and to further deception, which is not a happy place to be.

We are always mentally and emotionally aware of our daily spiritual *condition*. By contrast, the only time we are aware of our spiritual *position*, is when we read about it in the Bible. This assumes, of course, that we are already clear on what our spiritual position is. However, many Christians are not even aware of their spiritual position, let alone clear about it. As a result, these Christians have a view of Christianity that is primarily defined by their daily experiences. That causes a limited and restricting view of God, grace, and the possibilities of the Christian life.

If we have little or no understanding of our spiritual *position* in Christ, we are easily persuaded to believe our fellowship with God, and even the assurance of our salvation, *depends* on the quality of our daily walk and our spiritual condition. In the absence of other and better information about our forgiveness and *justification*, it is perfectly natural to make this sort of false assumption and to consequently entertain serious doubts about our spiritual progress and acceptability to God.

Throughout most people's lives, personal worth is determined by our performance according to the expectations and demands of others. We would be absolutely correct in saying that a natural or secular person is justified or judged by their works. Consequently, if we are not taught differently as Christians, we will simply continue to carry these secular practices and beliefs along with us. This will inevitably lead to some very heavy 'baggage' for us to carry and it can easily turn our Christian experience into a virtual nightmare.

Remember, if you, even as a Christian, take a hard, honest look inside yourself, you will never be very happy over what you find. If you are also looking within yourself to *feel* saved, or to *feel* righteous and spiritual, you will *always* be disappointed**!!** No one can build a stable, useful and Godly life, if we are attempting to build it on a foundation of error. [See Matthew 7:24-27]

CLIMBING OUT OF A LION'S MOUTH

Think about yourself, or perhaps some people you know who are trying to hide their disappointment and perceived failure in the anonymity of a large congregation, or trying to escape their inner turmoil through the 'feel-good' emotional warmth of a Praise and Worship experience, or are hiding behind the smoke screen of Christian activity. These things may grant us a temporary respite from our pain and insecurity, but we probably already know those 'good' feelings don't last. The only way to avoid a lot of unnecessary suffering and misery is if we know where to look for the assurance of our *salvation* and our complete acceptance by God. And hopefully now you do know!

The assurance we all need with regard to the full and complete acceptance of our lost and sinful souls by a holy, righteous and loving God is found in the Bible! Every day, regardless of how we may *feel* about ourselves or how poorly we or others think we are doing as Christians, we are always acceptable to God because we have been justified. We *know* this is true because the Bible "tells us so," not because we can see it or feel it.

The truth is, because Jesus paid the penalty for our sins, God can dismiss the charges and put the *righteousness* of Christ to our account. It is just like taking a person who is soiled and ragged, and then covering them with the most expensive and most beautiful cloak ever made. Now he appears fit to be a king, or the son of a King, but underneath he is still soiled and ragged. Look in the 'mirror' of the Word. We may still be dirty and ragged underneath, but just like Adam and Eve in the Garden, our 'nakedness', or shameful appearance, has been covered by God. This is what *justification* **is.** [See Romans 4:7-8 and Revelation 7:13-17]

What *sanctification* **does,** is to start cleaning up the dirty fellow underneath the beautiful cloak. And, like everyone else, our 'dirty fellow' will need many 'baths' over the course of his lifetime. But dirty or clean, he and we will always be covered with beautiful, clean cloaks of righteousness, and he and we will always remain the adopted children of the King! After all, when a child gets dirty, and they all do with frequency, it is cause for a bath, not for being disinherited and kicked back out on the streets, or sent back to an orphanage.

PHASE THREE: WE ARE FINALLY GLORIFIED

The third and final phase of our *salvation* is *glorification.* It occurs either when we die, or for some of us, at the rapture of the Church. The purpose of this final phase of our salvation, our *glorification*, is deliverance from the **PRESENCE** of sin! Think about it. First, the PENALTY of sin is dealt with. We never need to feel guilty again! Then God starts dealing with the POWER of sin in our lives, gradually loosening sin's hold on us so that we can grow spiritually. Then finally, when we have run the race and finished the course God set before us, He GLORIFIES us. Finally, we get away from even the PRESENCE of sin to dwell in the PRESENCE of the Lord forever. [Observe this pattern of salvation in Psalms 23!]

There are other wonderful passages that refer to our future in God's glory. For example, John 14:1-3 says, "Let not your heart be troubled; believe in God, believe also in Me. In my Father's house are many dwelling places [literally "rooms"]; if it were not so, I would have told you; for I go to prepare a place for you. And if I go to prepare a place for you, I will come again, and receive you to Myself; that where I am, there you may be also." Or I Corinthians 2:9 "but just as it is written, 'Things which eye has not seen and ear has not heard, and which have not entered the heart of man, all that God has prepared for those who love Him.'"

TRYING TO AVOID CONFUSION

To begin with, never forget, if *salvation* is by *grace through faith*, not works, then all three aspects or parts of our *salvation* are by *grace through faith*. This means we are always *justified* by *grace through faith*, not works, we are always being *sanctified* by *grace through faith*, not works, and we will always be *glorified* by *grace through faith*, not works!

Another way to think of these three parts of our salvation is to remember that as a Christian our *justification* has already occurred. So think of *justification* as salvation **PAST.** Currently, every Christian is being *sanctified* because this is an ongoing process for the rest of our lives. So think of *sanctification* as salvation **PRESENT**. And still waiting to happen is the last and final stage of our *salvation*. This will not occur until we pass away, so think of *glorification* as salvation **FUTURE.** Now we have a complete salvation. It cleanses our *past*, heals our *present*, and guarantees our *future*.

Although the plan of salvation as presented above is completely accurate, with its past, present, and future aspects, it is presented as you or I view it from a *human* perspective. For us, there is a past, present, and a future to our salvation. Frequently God looks at and describes things in the Bible from our perspective, which is bound by time and space, but sometimes God also describes things from His perspective, which is *eternal*. When God does speak about things from His perspective, we must remember that eternity has no past, present, or future. Eternity simply *is*.

For example, sometimes the Bible will present all of the aspects of our salvation in the past tense. In Romans 8:30 we were *"predestined"*, *"called"*, *"justified"* and *"glorified."* These are all mentioned in the same verse and all are referred to in the past tense, yet we just said that being *"glorified"* will happen in the future. What's more, *"sanctification"* is not even mentioned, while *"predestined"* and *"called"* appear to have been *added* to the plan of salvation.

Another example is found in I Corinthians 6:11 where we are referred to as *"washed"*, *"sanctified"*, and *"justified."* Now, not only has the order of two of the phases of our salvation [justified and sanctified] been *reversed*, again all of the phases mentioned are in the past tense. Moreover, now *glorified* is absent while another element, *washed*, has been added.

The reason God can and sometimes does speak of our salvation entirely in the past tense is because our salvation has already been completed and secured from God's viewpoint. His view is eternal while we are still down here trapped by time and space, slogging through the 'mud' of human existence. God sees us as a finished and completed work from the beginning, and this is something we need to learn to 'see' about ourselves too. [See Colossians 3:1-3]

This also means no matter how bad things may *look* to us, it is nevertheless all going to work out exactly according to God's plan. Therefore, God often speaks of our salvation as a completed work because He guarantees that it is, and we are told this to encourage us, not to confuse or discourage us. [See Romans 8:28; Philippians 1:6; I Thessalonians 5:24]

ELLIPTICAL STATEMENTS

An *ellipsis* refers to the omission of a word or words not necessary for the comprehension of a sentence. For example, we know that

Ephesians 2:8 teaches that we have been saved by grace through faith. This very clearly means that God's grace is what saves us.

On the other hand, faith saves no one. If it did, then we would have a salvation by works. However, we also know that we can only accept saving grace by faith, never by works of merit or by trying to earn it. Once it has been clearly explained so that we understand that salvation is a work of God, not man, and that both the grace that accomplished our salvation and the faith we need to receive it are both gifts from God [Ephesians 2:8-9], it is not necessary to repeat the entire formula and explanation **every** time faith or grace is mentioned.

Therefore, when it is said that we are saved by faith, we must remember this is an *elliptical* statement. Galatians 3:24 says, "Therefore the Law has become our tutor to lead us to Christ, that we may be justified by faith." Of course what we are to understand is that we are "justified by grace through faith." Since we already understand this, it is not necessary to repeat the entire phrase on every occasion. We are supposed to know that only the grace of God actually saves and justifies us.

For the same reason, it is not necessary to mention all three phases of our salvation every time it is referred to in the Bible. If a passage, such as Romans 8:30 only mentions "justified" and "glorified," this does not mean "sanctified" has suddenly been eliminated from the plan of salvation. It just means we are looking at another *elliptical* statement.

SUBSTITUTION AND ELABORATION

Another thing Scripture does is use the terms *justification, sanctification*, and *glorification* **interchangeably** with the word *salvation*. This is completely valid because as we recently explained, *justification, sanctification*, and *glorification* are the three components or phases of *salvation*.

An interesting example of this is found in Philippians 2:12-13 where we are told to *work* out our *"salvation."* After everything that has been said about grace and faith being *opposed* to works, now it sounds very much like we are being told that *salvation* is not only by works, but it is also accompanied by fear and trembling, suggesting a high degree of uncertainty. If we are only comparing verses where the word "salvation" appears, we become confused. But when we compare every verse that mentions one or more of all four of these important words, understanding that *salvation, justification, sanctification*, and *glorification* are sometimes used interchangeably, then this verse makes perfectly good and Biblically consistent sense.

So we substitute the word "*sanctification*" here for "*salvation*," and read this passage in context, which includes the next verse telling us that "God is at work in you, both to will and to do of His good pleasure," we end up with an important truth that is completely logical and in harmony with the rest of the Bible. Now Philippians 2:12-13 is teaching us that although the sanctification part of our salvation can be really tough and full of uncertainty at times, we must never forget God is always at work within us, giving us not only the desire to do His will, but also the ability. Consequently, we can face this part of our salvation [sanctification] with confidence.

In Romans 8:30 and again in I Corinthians 6:11 we also have examples of what we could call elaboration. "*Predestined*," "*called*" and "*washed*" all serve to elaborate or give us more information, in this case about our "*justification*." These terms do not change the meaning of "*justification*;" they help to explain or enhance it, as well as to enhance the meaning of grace!

THE '*UNPLAN*' FOR SALVATION

We will always be faced with efforts to mix *Law* and *grace* together. This happens whenever the Word of God encounters some form of secularism or secular philosophy combined with what we humans like to refer to as our 'common sense' or reason. There is nothing sensible or reasonable about a human's common sense, since it is always based on some form of secular belief.

Whether it comes from Pelagius, Arminius or Locke,[the names are not important] what is important are the erroneous ideas being put forth as being biblical, when the fact is that Satan is *always* behind them. In every case, the end result is that the force of God's pure Holy Word is diluted with the impure forces of human reasoning and ignorance.

Once something is polluted, the only question that remains is not if but how badly is it polluted?

Fortunately, Law and grace can *not* be mixed together. Unfortunately, whenever mixing Law and grace is tried, and it is constantly being tried, we *always* end up with some form of **legalism** because grace is only grace as long as it remains *pure* grace. If it is not pure, it is not grace at all. God's grace plus *absolutely nothing* equals God's grace.

We should also remember that *legalism* and the *works* of the Law are the *default setting* for human reasoning. This means every time we faulty humans try to add to or take away something from God's pure sovereign grace, we always end up taking away or losing some of the joy and confidence of our salvation.

Additionally, because of this so-called default setting in secular humankind, we humans do not turn to or discover grace by accident. We are simply not able to naturally comprehend God's grace. It is foolishness to the natural man. Understanding and embracing God's grace always requires the purposeful work of the Holy Spirit working in and through a regenerated, being renewed, Biblically informed mind.[13] We should never be surprised at or discouraged by the resistance we encounter in trying to communicate the truth about God's grace. It is and always will be Law *versus* grace, not Law *and* grace. What now follows are some of the common errors that have resulted from trying to mix the unmixable. Naturally, they directly concern the gospel and God's plan of salvation. And remember, if we do not have grace & faith + nothing, all we have is nothing!

THE FLAWED, SECULAR, HUMANISTIC PLAN OF SALVATION

Many Christians honestly believe and are even taught that we have some degree of responsibility for our salvation. Of course, because of the old 'default setting', the arguments for this position really do seem reasonable to our earthly minds. For example, it seems reasonable to believe that all humans have complete freedom of choice and because of this God is holding us responsible for either accepting or rejecting Him. It is further maintained that if we did not have freedom of choice, then God would have no right to judge us or hold us accountable.

Some will choose to accept Jesus as their Savior, others will not. We hear appeals to accept, receive, or claim Jesus as your Lord and Savior all the time in church; we read it in books, we see it on Christian T. V., and we hear it on Christian radio. It must be true. After all, I make lots of choices every day. So is there a problem? Yes, but only if we read the Bible [In this case read Romans 9].

The root of the problem is that salvation has *now* become a matter of grace **plus** making the *right* choice. It is no longer up to God alone, but now it is up to God and me. And if I fail or refuse to make the correct choice, God will not be able to save me. And in most cases, without even realizing what we have done, we have actually reduced God's role in salvation to that of a bystander who originally set this salvation thing in motion, but now it is a take it or leave it proposition.

This defective line of reasoning is consistently taught throughout today's Evangelical movement, and no one seems to realize that God's sovereignty and power have been rendered subservient to our freedom to choose. Is this not putting man on the throne of our lives in place of God? Is this not an insidiously offensive way to treat our glorious Lord? Is this not a way to cripple every Christian who is sold this secular bill of goods? Does this not sound like Satan winning a significant round in the battle for the souls and minds of men?

Consequently, when we experience sin and failure, if we have been convinced that our sins and failures are our responsibility because we were told to make the right choices and we did not make the right choices, then the burden for our sins and failures ends up resting on our shoulders, rather than on the cross *where they belong*! Repeated confession never seems to relieve the burden because we put it there in the first place. As far as God is concerned, it is already forgiven.

Telling a struggling or failing Christian if he or she wants God's help they will *first* need to change course, clean up, and get their spiritual 'house in order,' is like having a combat medic tell a wounded soldier if he can manage to bandage his wound and then crawl to the field hospital he will then be given aid. Thankfully, this is *not* how combat medics operate and this is most certainly not how God's grace works; not to mention that this doctrinal distortion is not even remotely Biblical!

There is another problem with grace *plus* making the right choice. If we are saved by making the right choice, we will always have something to *brag* about, because we made the right choice, whereas others did not. Remember, God says with regard to our salvation, we have absolutely **nothing** to brag about [I Corinthians 1:26-31!!]!

Another way that grace is quickly displaced is in the debates over the proper modes of baptism. Some say we must be sprinkled, some want to have water poured over them, and many others argue for full immersion. It is actually taught in some Christian circles that the proper mode of water baptism determines whether you are saved or not. Other extreme groups insist that unless one is baptized with the Holy Spirit evidenced by speaking in tongues, they are not saved. The more tolerant advocates of speaking in tongues will only consign you to second class Christian citizenship if you do not speak in tongues.

Here again, we now have grace **plus** something. Whether it is the proper mode of water baptism or the proper mode of spirit baptism, when we add anything to *by grace through faith*, the emphasis will *always* end up on you and me and on our doing the right thing, not on God and simply believing in and trusting what He has already done for us!

God is very clear on this matter so let's see what the Scriptures really say:

Romans 3:19-24: "Now we know that whatever the Law says, it speaks to those who are under the Law, that every mouth may be closed, and all the world may become accountable to God; because by the works of the Law no flesh will be justified in His sight; for through the Law comes the knowledge of sin. But now apart from the Law the righteousness of God has been manifested, being witnessed by the Law and the Prophets; even the righteousness of God through faith in Jesus Christ for all those who believe; for there is no distinction; for all have sinned and fall short of the glory of God, being justified as a gift by His grace through the redemption which is in Christ Jesus;"

Romans 3:27-28: "Where then is boasting? It is excluded. By what kind of law? Of works? No, but by a law of faith. For we maintain that a man is justified by faith apart from works of the Law."

John 6:29: "This is the work of God, that you believe in Him whom He has sent."

It should be very clear to us that we really have nothing to offer God but our sinful souls. On the other hand, God has *everything* to offer us. There is no work we can perform save one, which according to John 6:29 is to simply *believe* in Jesus! Faith, repentance, confession, surrender, restitution, and humility are all part of the salvation process, but they are results, not causes. These are all elements of our response to the grace of God, not works that cause God's grace to start operating, and these responses, including faith, are supplied by God through his Holy Spirit when we need them! [See Ephesians 2:8-9; Romans 3:21-31; Luke 18:9-14]

So beware if you have something to boast about in your salvation. If you ever entertain thoughts like "well, at least I made the right choice," or "I know I'm saved because I was properly baptized," **beware**; know that you are embracing that fatally flawed, legalistic, secular state of mind that wants to say, "Hey, I'm not so bad. I was just *wounded*."

THE OTHER FLAWED, SECULAR, HUMANISTIC PLAN OF SALVATION

In certain Christian circles it is taught that even though you have been forgiven, you can still *lose* your salvation by sinning again. This is a logically consistent conclusion if we are indeed subject to a salvation that requires the exercise of the free will of a person who has been wounded by sin, but not killed. After all, if you were really dead in your sins, you would not have a will left to exercise let alone anything else now would you?

Moreover, they maintain that if you were to die before you repented of whatever sin caused the loss of your salvation, you would go straight to hell. Many other Christians do not accept losing one's salvation as a valid doctrine. They claim to believe in eternal security [once saved, always saved], but at the same time they also accept a doctrine of free will. Not having a solid basis for their professed belief in eternal security, they are really expressing a hope more than a known certainty that they are eternally secure.

There will always be some who will try to teach you that the Christian life is an ongoing cycle of losing one's salvation, repenting and regaining one's salvation, until the next time you sin.

The motive behind this false belief includes a desire to force heightened morality among believers and the felt need by many Christian leaders to retain greater control over their congregations for their protection. However, this *'infernal insecurity'* always breeds spiritual immaturity and instability, which in turn discourages, not encourages, individual evangelism.[14]

Others will teach two plans of salvation. The first plan is that we are justified by grace through faith alone, and even that it is an eternally secure gift. However, once saved the second plan of salvation kicks in, basically teaching that a Christian's sanctification is lived and governed by laws, rules, and keeping the Ten Commandments. So here we are given, incorrectly of course, one basis for *justification* and an entirely different basis for *sanctification*. This again is a toxic, deadly mix of grace and faith *combined* with works of the Law because those who should know better don't. Instead of realizing they have embraced two systems that are diametrically opposed to each another, this foul amalgamation is taught and believed by many.

Moreover once we turn to rules, laws, and steps [or whatever you want to call legalism], we will also resort to self-effort. Grace and faith get left far behind and, despite the occasional mention of the words, forgotten.[15] Add to all of this the fact that sometimes we do not even realize we are sinning, at least not right away, and you have a 'perfect' recipe for insecurity, misery, inaction and futility.

Likewise, if our beginning sense of forgiveness has been marred by subsequent doubt and uncertainty, our time on earth will not be happily spent. If we are worried about whether God is pleased or displeased with us, the chances of our taking some risky and significant steps of faith for God are going to be *slim* and *none*. The possible results will just not seem worth the risk of failure, our lives will bear little fruit for God, and it *will* even make it easier for others to control and manipulate us. [Please read Matthew 13:58, John 15:1-5, and Galatians 4:17]

O FOOLISH GALATIANS

The seriousness of trying to mix the pure and complete plan of salvation with legalism caused the vexation and hearty condemnation of the Apostle Paul. Twice in three verses, he calls his Galatian audience *"foolish."* In Galatians 3:1-3 Paul's righteous indignation is directed at Christians who teach or believe they are saved by grace through faith, but are now being sanctified by the flesh, that is, by works of the Law. One can only wish with Paul, that these legalistic teachers "…would even mutilate themselves." [Galatians 5:12]

The reason for Paul's indignation, and hopefully ours, is over what legalism does to a Christian's life. *Justification*, the first phase of our salvation, is intended to give us the assurance and confidence we need to bear fruit for God. The assurance we gain from our *justification* is the 'soil' in which God plants the seeds for our growth, or *sanctification*. The greater our assurance is, the better the 'soil' is, and the better the fruit that grows from it. [Take a read in Jeremiah 32:38-41]

Those who hold to and teach legalism scoff at those of us who believe that once saved means always saved. They do not seem to realize they are denying us and themselves the dignity and magnificence of being totally justified and declared righteous for all eternity by God Himself, and trying to replace this with the puny self-effort of man. They are completely missing the incredible beauty, logic, and balance at work in God's plan of salvation, not to mention the clearly revealed teaching of Scripture!

IT IS WRITTEN

It is written in the Gospel of John 6:37-39; 44; and 65; "All that the Father gives Me shall come to Me; and the one who comes to Me I will certainly not cast out. For I have come down from heaven, not to do My own will, but the will of Him who sent Me. And this is the will of Him who sent Me, that of all He has given Me I lose nothing, but raise it up on the last day." "No one can come to Me, unless the Father who sent Me draws him; and I will raise him up on the last day." "And He was saying, 'For this reason I have said to you, that no one can come to Me, unless it has been granted him from the Father.'"

In John 10:27-30 we read, "My sheep hear My voice and I know them, and they follow Me; and I give eternal life to them; and they shall never perish, and no one shall snatch them out of the Father's hand. I and the Father are one."

And never forget the wonderful encouragement of Philippians 1:6: "For I am confidant of this very thing, that He who began a good work in you [justification] will perfect it [sanctification] until the day of Christ Jesus [glorification]." There are similar statements in I Thessalonians 5:24 and Hebrews 13:20-21. Other passages I would suggest you study are Matthew 13:24-30 then 36-43, Romans 8:29-39, Romans 9:14-24, Romans 11:1-7 and 29, I Corinthians 1:22-31, and 3:10-15.

Every Christian has a deep and desperate need for the *assurance* that they are fully loved, fully forgiven and fully accepted by God just as they are. *Assurance* is defined as "1. A pledge or a promise: a declaration that inspires or is intended to inspire confidence; 2. Confidence in your ability or status; 3. Freedom from uncertainty; 4. ...overcoming doubt." [16]

Think about the emotional and psychological freedom we can have when we are fully assured of God's unconditional love, forgiveness, patience, and acceptance. When our minds dwell on what God has done, then we have confidence in our status as one of God's chosen to be adopted children. We are free from any uncertainty about who we are, where we came from, what we should be doing, or where we are headed when we die. There is absolutely no basis in Scripture for ever doubting all that God has done for us, is doing in us, and will continue to do forever. [Please see Romans 8:28-39; Ephesians 1:3-14, 18-23; 2:1-10] Then think about what we would be missing if the legalists were correct. Aren't you glad they are wrong?

Chapter Six
BLESSED ASSURANCE

GUILTY AS SIN

If the human race knows anything at all, it knows we would all be a lot happier if we never had to experience *guilt*. Apart from sociopaths and psychopaths, no one is exempt from experiencing *guilt*. Not surprisingly, helping people deal with guilt has become a big business in our culture. Psychiatrists use medications, psychologists use psychoanalysis, counselors counsel, and self-help books abound, all part of the effort to 'free' us from guilt and its consequences. Filling people up with tranquilizers or helping them to 'rationalize' their behavior may provide them with some temporary relief from their deep-seated awareness of guilt, but neither medication, psychoanalysis, or counseling will ever produce the freedom we want and *need*.

The reason is simple; the *cause* of guilt is <u>un</u>forgiven sin and nothing else. Guilt is either the result of a sin, or the result of something that we *think* is a sin. In other words, sometimes we really are guilty, and sometimes we just think we are guilty, but in either case we will feel and act guilty. The guilt can diminish or disappear only when we deal correctly with the cause.

Moreover, guilt really is a *fact* not a *feeling*, even though we are fond of saying "I feel guilty." The reason guilt is not a feeling is because a feeling is amoral, that is, feelings are neither right nor wrong they just are. What we call 'feeling guilty' is neither right nor wrong, but it is darned uncomfortable and for some it can become unbearable.

The question of morality enters into the equation when we *act* on what we are feeling. One example of this is found in Ephesians 4:26

which says, "Be angry, and yet do not sin; do not let the sun go down on your anger, and do not give the devil an opportunity." Anger is a very specific feeling; when you feel anger you won't mistake it for anything else. However, our passage makes it very clear that a person can be angry and yet not sin, because feelings are neither right nor wrong, they just are. But holding onto my anger, in other words letting the sun set on it" is an action on my part, it will give Satan an opening, and this is when anger becomes sin.

Likewise, all the feelings we lump together under the label *guilt* are neither right nor wrong, they just are. How we act or react to these feelings is very much a moral issue. If I ignore guilt it is sin; if I do works to compensate for my guilt and sin it is a sin. When I lay my guilt and sin at the altar of God's grace, obviously this is not sin but is the right and correct [and only] thing we can do with our guilt and sin.

Feelings of guilt begin when we become conscious and convicted of committing a sin. We may have broken God's Law or failed to do something God has commanded. These are also known as *sins of commission* and *sins of omission*. However, someone unfamiliar with the Bible who does not believe in God and is simply not 'listening' can be quite guilty of sinning and not realize it consciously, though I believe we all know we are guilty at some subconscious level. The divine process that makes me aware of my guilt and its cause is called *conviction,* which is something only the Holy Spirit of God can correctly do.

Along with the conviction of sin come some very unpleasant feelings. Some of the feelings *resulting* from guilt are shame, remorse, embarrassment, and self-reproach. We humans will find the feelings associated with guilt so intolerable that we will either surrender to God or start making all sorts of excuses, and 'manufacture' all sorts of camouflage or compensations to hide our guilt not only from those around us but even from ourselves.[17]

This was certainly the case with Adam and Eve when their eyes were opened and they made coverings out of fig leaves and then hid from God when they heard Him coming [cf. Genesis 3:6-8]. This is also why evolution emerged as an alternative belief system to creation, along with the philosophical fancy that all humans are basically good and all 'bad' behavior stems from either nurture or one's social environment.

The word *evil* doesn't really exist in the world's vocabulary, although 9/11 and the war on terror is starting to change this.

Most, *not all*, but most mental health professionals are not informed or equipped to deal with the issue of unforgiven sin, and most do not even acknowledge the existence of real guilt or sin. The only valid way to dispose of a person's guilt is by the cross of Jesus Christ. The difficulty with this approach is that the guilty person must admit to themselves and to God what they are guilty of and they have to be willing to have God change them [again refer to Adam & Eve], which is a lot easier said than done. Moreover, for many mental health professionals this would obviously result in a lot less income. In fact, it would probably put them in the same income bracket as pastors.

Nevertheless, for all their ineffective efforts, the psychologists, psychiatrists, and counselors still manage to write best-selling books, acquire fame and recognition, and make lots of money. The patients, however, usually with much lighter wallets, are still carrying around their burdens. "A rose by any other name is still a rose," said Mr. Shakespeare. Sin by any other name is still sin, and guilt by any other name is still guilt, and *nothing* but the blood of Jesus will wash away my sins. If we aren't directing people to Christ, we are part of the problem, not the solution.

Actually, there are two ways to remove guilt. In both cases, it begins with the Bible, the word of God. The Bible tells us what is not acceptable to God, which is sin, and explains the plan of salvation. Conviction of sin by the Spirit of God leads to repentance and regeneration [being born again]. However, if I have guilt over something that is *not* a sin, again only the Bible can tell me this. In this case, Biblical knowledge will enable me to escape *false* guilt by rejecting it.

Mankind has invented many excuses, rationalizations, and behaviors which produce partial or temporary relief from the conviction that we are guilty of sin, but it is impossible to make sin and guilt fully disappear apart from the only means prescribed by God in the Bible. The solution to sin and guilt is forgiveness and *justification!*

VIVA LA DIFFERENCE!

As we discovered in the last chapter, God's plan of salvation consists of three phases, justification, sanctification and glorification. These three phases occur in a specific order; first comes justification, which delivers us from the *penalty* of sin. Next is the process of our sanctification, which gradually delivers us from the *power* of sin, and finally our glorification, which delivers us from the *presence* of sin.

There are three incredibly important principles we need to remember about the *difference* between being *sanctified* and being *justified*. Many Christians today have no idea what these principles are; let alone why they are so important to understand!

First, the sanctification process begins as soon as a person has been justified and continues until the day they go to be with Jesus. Justification and sanctification are not even close to being the same thing.

Second, sanctification is an ongoing process, a work in progress, and never finds completion in this life, whereas *justification* occurs and is completed in a moment of time.

Third, our progress in sanctification has no bearing whatsoever on the status of our relationship with God. The status of our relationship with God is determined only by our justification, which you may recall includes our being accounted or declared (not *made*) righteous.

These first two phases of our salvation, justification and sanctification, take place *during* our earthly lifetime. For this reason, they are of greater concern and importance to us now, and our failure to correctly understand these first two phases of salvation will cause us a lot of unnecessary confusion and strife in our daily lives

Before we were justified, sin always separated us from God. Since we have been *justified*, nothing can ever separate us from God again. Romans 8:38-39 emphatically and eloquently states this vital truth; "For I am convinced that neither death, nor life, nor angels, nor principalities, nor things present, nor things to come, nor powers, nor depth, nor any other created thing [which includes ourselves], shall be able to separate us from the love of God, which is in Christ Jesus our Lord." *We must constantly remind ourselves and each other the unchanging truth that once we are justified, God is no longer our Judge, but our Father.* This is essential knowledge when we are mired down in the mud of our daily lives, and think we couldn't be dirtier.

HAVING TO GO WHERE ANGELS FEAR TO TREAD

This truth also becomes all the more important when we realize that we live on a *battlefield*. It is in our daily lives where the war between Christianity and the forces of evil continues to be fought, and it is where our *sanctification* takes place. These battles are fought over ideas and beliefs, which means the objective of the battle is to win the *minds* of mankind, including your mind and mine. One would have thought that it would be a battle for man's will, but the simple fact is that our choices always result from our most deeply held beliefs. How we think will determine what we choose, which is exactly why the devil is trying to capture our minds and bend them, as much as possible, to his way of thinking.

In Ephesians, the Apostle Paul draws on the analogy of a Roman soldier's armor, shield, and weapon as a means of teaching us about this battle we are in and how to survive it.[18] Ephesians 6:10-13 tells us this: "Finally, be strong in the Lord, and in the strength of His might. Put on the full armor of God, that you may be able to stand firm against the schemes of the devil. For our struggle is not against flesh and blood, but against the rulers, against the powers, against the world forces of this darkness, against the spiritual forces of wickedness in the heavenly places. Therefore take up the full armor of God, that you may be able to resist in the evil day, and having done everything, to stand firm."

Like it or not, every Christian is engaged in this spiritual war, and like all good soldiers, we learn to hate war, but this doesn't mean giving in to the enemy's forces and strategies. We may not see bomb craters on our battlefield, but I guarantee that there are daily **casualties** in this war, and most of them will be 'head' wounds.

We will all be wounded from time to time, but don't be discouraged! There are no fatalities for those in God's army [after all, He did grant us eternal life]. And since all of us will show up in heaven with our share of spiritual Purple Hearts, we need to pay careful attention to what the Holy Spirit has written for us here in the Scriptures.

BECOMING A CASUALTY

One of the things the Spirit of God does for us in bringing us to salvation is to change how we think and what we believe. Some of these necessary changes in our thinking are neither instantaneous nor complete in every area and detail. Even after we become born-again Christians, we will still be affected by the secular world's belief system which surrounds us, and to some degree still indwells us. It is for precisely this reason that Romans 12:2a warns us, saying, "And do not be conformed to this world, but be transformed by the renewing of your mind." The word "conformed" literally means to be pressed into a mold.

To make matters worse, Revelations 12:10 refers to the "accuser" of the brethren, "who accuses them before our God day and night." The devil's accusations have one simple goal; to convince us we are worthless *guilty* sinners and therefore useless to God. I Peter 5:8 warns us, "Be of sober spirit, be on the alert. Your adversary, the devil, prowls about like a roaring lion, seeking someone to devour." The most effective way to take a big bite out of a Christian's effectiveness, short of death, is with *guilt*. Obviously it works, because the devil accuses us before God 24/7.

The lies Satan whispers in our ears about our failure as Christians, our utter worthlessness because we still sin, and the unlikely possibility that God could love or use someone like us are intended to wound us and render us incapable of continuing the battle. However, we can begin to avoid living our lives under a cloud of guilt and secular conformity by learning what God has actually said in the Bible. The antidote to the poisons of guilt and secularism begins with the truth or doctrine of justification. We have to learn to counter the lies we are told with the truth we should already know.

SHOOTING OUR WOUNDED

Some of the more serious casualties will strike Christians who are not adequately protected by an understanding of God's grace. Ephesians 6:14-18 lists the various items of 'armor' God has provided for our protection. It begins by girding up our minds with the *truth* of God's Word, particularly on the subject of grace and the fact that we have already been fully justified. Learn how to put on your armor, and learn how to use your 'sword' properly, and how to always rely on it. "All Scripture is inspired [literally God breathed] by God and profitable for teaching, for reproof, for correction, for training in righteousness; that the man of God may be adequate, equipped for every good work." [And equipped for every battle] II Timothy 3:16-17

It is tragic but true that Christians are the *only* army in the world who 'shoot' their own wounded. Typically this is done with guilt fueled by *legalism*! So here is an important warning for every Christian: We need to be very careful with regard to who we let help diagnose our 'injuries' and prescribe remedies. Be certain what you are hearing and counting on is Biblical, consistent with The New Covenant of God's grace, and not merely someone's legalistic opinions.

To a wounded believer, suffering over some sin or failure in their life, pouring the acid of legalism into those wounds won't cure them; it will only make them worse. Legalism is brutal and cruel, and of absolutely no use in healing spiritual casualties or fostering spiritual growth. *Legalism* is often a cudgel found in the hands of those who are supposed to lead us but are instead striving to control us! *Our first line of defense is believing the truth about our justification, so get your shield up!*

BY GRACE THROUGH FAITH

God's plan for our salvation is based on a simple basic formula; we are saved by *grace* through *faith*. The gift of God's grace is the only cause of our salvation, and the gift of faith is the only response for our salvation. Both grace and faith are *gifts* given to us by God. Ephesians 2:8 clearly says, "For by grace you have been saved through faith; and that not of yourselves, it is the gift of God." There is no aspect of our salvation that we either deserve or have earned!

Any departure from this formula is a fatal error. Theologians have been debating the proper place or function of God's Laws for a person who is under God's grace since the First Century. Every time someone starts talking about not being under the Law since we are now under grace, Christians start getting nervous, and especially those who are responsible for oversight in the body of Christ. This continues to be an issue despite the many references in the New Testament to the fact that all believers are no longer under the Law but are now under grace.

One such example is found in Romans 3:28, which says, "For we maintain that a man is justified by faith apart from works of the Law."

Quite a few will allow that we are saved [justified] by grace, but maintain that our daily lives [sanctification] should be guided by the Law. Their belief is that keeping the Ten Commandments won't save us, but keeping them will sanctify us. Their problem is that we can't have two plans for salvation. We are sanctified by exactly the same means by which we are justified. Either it will be by keeping the Law, or it will be by grace through faith, but never both!

There is an underlying fear, particularly among church leaders, that teaching *by grace through faith alone* will lead to something called *antinomianism*. "Antinomianism (from the Greek αντι, "against" + νομος, "law"), or lawlessness (in the Greek Bible: ανομια,[1] which is ("unlawful"), in theology, is the idea that members of a particular religious group are under no obligation to obey the laws of ethics or morality as presented by religious authorities.

[2] Antinomianism is the polar opposite of legalism, which is the notion that obedience to a code of religious law is necessary for salvation.[19] Perhaps a more current definition can be found in the warning remarks made to me by a Pastor who told me that "teaching *by grace alone* would only lead to everyone just sliding around on their butts." I believe his definition is directed to the *worldly* need to maintain control over one's church flock. I always thought Jesus was in control!

According to the Lord, obedience to the Law or for that matter to any laws is called "works of the Law." There is some confusion about what constitutes a good work as opposed to a work of the Law. The simplest distinction is that any work performed by us to garner God's favor in some way is a work of the Law or a dead work. Any work that is performed in or through us by God, as we are trusting in His power and ability to do it, is a good work or work of faith.

Salvation is never based on our obedience to laws because grace is the cause, not the effect or result! Salvation can not be based on our efforts for this reason. There is only one cause for salvation, only one reason why you or I are saved, and the cause and reason for salvation is God's grace, and only God's grace. God's grace is His gift to us, not His reward for a job well done

The only reason I know without a doubt that I am acceptable to God, mud and all, is by grace through faith. The only assurance I have that I will finish the race intact and go to God's heaven when I die is by grace through faith. The only way I can survive life's daily struggles is by grace through faith. There is no other way, and I am truly sorry there are so many books, even in Christian bookstores, that suggest there is some special plan or formulas for getting through this life unscathed, not to mention a few books that try to debunk the essential essence of grace and turn our sanctification into a constant effort on our part to keep God happy.

Despite whatever your favorite TV preacher or bartender may say about faith and works, this basic formula of *by grace through faith* is repeated throughout the New Testament. It may not always be popular or helpful in religious 'extortion,' but it is always true. The Apostle Paul paid particular attention to grace and faith in his epistles. Since the totality of our *salvation* is only by grace through faith, it must follow that the three phases of salvation, *justification, sanctification*, and *glorification*, are likewise only by grace through faith.

Justification occurs at a moment in time, when we initially put our faith in Christ for salvation. Glorification also occurs at a moment in time, the moment we die or if our timing is just right, at the rapture of the church. In between these two moments in our lives stretches the rest of our Christian experience. This is the period of our sanctification, and it is the most difficult part of our spiritual experience. Nevertheless, it is still by grace through faith, not by works.

Jesus spoke to Paul on the road to Damascus, telling him what had been determined for him in Acts 26:16-18; "But arise, and stand on your feet; for this purpose I have appeared to you, to appoint you a minister and a witness not only to the things which you have seen, but also to the things in which I will appear to you; delivering you from the Jewish people and from the Gentiles, to whom I am sending you, to open their eyes so that they may turn from darkness to light and from the dominion of Satan to God, in order that they may receive forgiveness of sins and an inheritance among those who have been sanctified by faith in Me."

During this period of sanctification, which literally means being set apart for God's exclusive use, we encounter our many shortcomings, the hard lessons of faith, and the endless assaults by the devil. One of the main weapons in our arsenal is "the sword of the Spirit, which is the word of God [Ephesians 6:17]." The doctrine or truth of justification is what tempers the steel of this sword. Every follower of Christ will find many occasions to apply the truth of their justification in their daily lives [which is the sanctification part]. Living a stable, secure life with Christ depends heavily on how well we understand what justification means to us personally!

THE WONDER OF JUSTIFICATION

Let us assume that you, the reader, have been led to enter by that narrow gate that leads to life, and you have been forgiven all of your sins. The forgiveness of your sin is by *grace* alone through the sacrifice of our Lord Jesus on Calvary's cross as the full payment for sin. You have received this forgiveness by *faith* and have therefore been justified before God. This is the backdrop to Christ's words in Matthew 11:28-29, where He says, "Come to Me, all who are weary and heavy laden, and I will give you rest. Take My yoke upon you, and learn from Me, for I am gentle and humble in heart; and you shall find rest for your souls. For My yoke is easy, and My load is light." What follows now are some of the results that *justification* accomplishes in every Christian's life.

There are *three* very good reasons why our 'loads' should be light. First, God has *forgiven* all our lawless deeds. We are not just talking about mistakes here; we are also talking about the evil deeds we went out of our way to commit [*sins & trespasses*]. When the Scriptures say our sin is forgiven, it means all of our sins, past, present, and future.

Justification means never having to answer for your sins and trespasses before God the Judge. The penalty has been paid and the prisoners [you and me] have been legally set free. We no longer have any right to bear the burden of guilt on our shoulders, for God has removed our guilt through Christ on the cross.

The second thing God has done for us is to *cover over* all of our sins. The word used here for *sin* is from the Greek *harmartia*, at whose root is the idea of shooting at and *missing* a target. Failure is always embarrassing, and we who have failed hate being reminded of it. For those of us who are in Christ, not only has the penalty been paid, but God has covered up our sins, meaning He is not going to bring them up again or hold them over our heads. God is not going to embarrass us, now or in the future.

Justification also forgives and covers both sins of *omission,* which are the sins I committed by accident or by not doing the things I know I should have and sins of *commission,* which are sins I committed knowingly on purpose. All of our sins are forgiven and covered completely, that is, for all those who receive the justification that is the free gift of God's grace through faith.

The third thing God has done by justifying us is that He will never take our sins into *account.* God has forgiven our sins, covered them over, and will never dig them back up and hold them against us. If you are a born-again Christian then you are no longer a sinner. We believers have no right to refer to ourselves as sinners except in the past tense. We were sinners but we have been saved by grace through faith. Now we are saints.

Moreover, we who are in Christ [saved saints] have also been *reckoned* or accounted as *righteous* before God. Notice that this does *not* say *made righteous*; it says *declared or accounted righteous.* Imagine standing before a group of people and being covered with a perfectly white sheet. Because it covers you completely, those who are looking at you only see the purity of the white sheet. This is how God now sees each of us who have been justified from a *judicial* viewpoint.

From a *practical* standpoint, the one who has been covered with the sheet is no different by being covered. He is the same old dirty rascal as before. This is where each Christian is at the moment we are justified; we are covered so that the observer who looks at us [God] sees only the perfect righteousness of Christ Himself.

Underneath the sheet we are still badly soiled and in need of a lot of cleansing. This is where sanctification begins, and we remember that sanctification is a *process* that continues until we go to be with God. If we forget the fact that we are already justified, if we fail to hang onto this absolutely necessary truth, then the constant cleansing process will continue reminding us of just how soiled we really are and soon it will have us questioning how a perfect God could ever accept or put up with the likes of us. The fastest freeway route to doubt and guilt is to *forget* our justification!

THE GUARANTEES OF JUSTIFICATION

There are three *guarantees* God gives us with regard to our justification. First of all, He has *guaranteed* us that there is a *specific purpose* and plan for each of our lives. Jesus says in John 10:10, that "I came that they [that's us!] might have life, and might have it abundantly." When I think of abundance as God means it, I always think of Luke 6:38, where Jesus said "Give, and it will be given to you; good measure, pressed down, shaken together, running over, they will pour into your lap." In Ephesians 2:10 God also says "For we are His workmanship, created in Christ Jesus for good works, which God prepared beforehand, that we should walk in them." (See also Romans 8:28-29, Philippians 1:6, 2:13, and I Thessalonians 5:24)

Whenever discussions arise concerning the will of God for our lives, we always tend to think of God's will in specific, individual terms, like it is a job description. What is God's plan for *MY* life? What does He want *ME* to do? What work has God planned for *ME*? There is often a lot of frustration associated with these questions, because the answers we want are not clear to us yet, and may not be for some time to come. First we need to get past the importance of *ME*.

It has been my experience that God is disinclined to let us know too much in advance. He really prefers that we *trust* Him as fully as possible, and *learn* to do this on a consistent basis. Besides, if you or I knew everything in advance, like God already does, we might be tempted to make some suggestions for 'changes' or 'improvements.' Instead, may I suggest a better way to look at the will of God for our lives?

God has already told us His will for our lives. He has told us His will in universal terms, teaching us what He wants every Christian to be and do. God has given us His will in the New Testament, for all of us to read and understand [See Matthew 28:18-20]. This already gives us more of His will than we could hope to accomplish in a lifetime. We would all be well advised to start here with His clearly revealed plan for each and every one of us, and trust the Holy Spirit to reveal God's specific will for each of us when His chosen time comes. I assure you God can and will do this for each of us, however I can't guarantee that you will always like it!

There are two more guarantees in John 6:37 and 39. I must confess I have had to cling to these two on many occasions. In verse 37 Jesus gives us the second promise guaranteed by our justification: "All that the Father gives Me shall come to Me; and the one who comes to Me I will certainly not cast out." Put in the plainest terms, it means God will *never* throw me away or get rid of me! I am secure in God's love and in His family because He really is my Father!

The third guaranteed promise made to us because we have been justified by God's incredible grace is in John 6:39: "And this is the will of Him who sent Me, that of all that He has given Me I lose nothing, but raise it up on the last day." Again in the plainest terms, God will not lose me or forget where He left me! Hang onto this promise when you feel like you have been stuck away on the last shelf in the back of the closet for years. He remembers where He put you, He knows why He put you there [even if we don't], and He knows when and how to get you, just like He did with Paul.

The apostle Paul was originally called Saul, a Pharisee, and he worked as an agent for the Sanhedrin, the Jew's ruling body in Jerusalem. His job was to round up and imprison and in some cases even execute Christians. On his way to Damascus, Paul was unquestionably con-verted to faith in God through the Son, our Lord Christ Jesus. His story can be read in Acts 9:1-31. The problem was, after his conversion, Paul stirred up so much strife with his preaching, that the Jews in Damascus started plotting to kill him. After his escape in the middle of the night, he went to Jerusalem and caused more problems. Finally, the Apostles in Jerusalem had had enough of his 'brand' of witnessing and sent Paul back to his home town of Tarsus to cool his heels.

For the next *thirteen* years Paul remained in Tarsus in total obscurity on the last shelf in the back of the closet, until Barnabus sought him out and brought Paul back to Jerusalem. The great Apostle Paul, the human God used to write half of the New Testament, spent thirteen years on the last shelf in the back of the closet. But God didn't forget about Paul, and He will never forget about any of us.

We are *all* part of the plan, guaranteed. God will never forget us, lose us, or throw us away; no matter how long we might have to wait on some shelf, or how deeply we have managed to bury ourselves in the mud! We have been *justified*. We have been *adopted*. We have been *declared righteous*. We have a *mission*, which we will not fail to accomplish in God's way and in God's time. And when we are finally finished, we will have a new home. It's all in the contract.

THE BENEFITS OF JUSTIFICATION

*** PEACE ***

One of the old jokes told about being a Pastor is that the pay isn't too good, but you can't beat the retirement benefits. Regardless of the work God gives us to do in this life, being called into God's forever family carries with it some amazing benefits.

I enjoy reading humorous bumper stickers, so I guess that means I am easily amused. Anyway, it is interesting to notice how many cars have bumper stickers extolling the virtues of *world peace*. The downside to these stickers is the grossly mistaken belief that if we stop shooting at *them*, they will be kind and reasonable enough to stop shooting at *us*. There is this simplistic belief that if we disarm, everyone else will too. Then, of course, there would be world peace.

However, this irrational 'belief' fails to take into account the fact that throughout history humans have always been at war. This 'belief' also ignores the existence of evil and the fallen sinful nature of the human race. Until evil is eradicated along with man's fallen nature, wars will continue, and anyone who disarms will certainly lose those wars and probably their lives.

Nevertheless, peace at an individual level will always be welcome to us. Just the lessening of strife and fear in a person's life can add years to that life and better health throughout those years.

Romans 5:1 tells us that having been justified by grace through faith, we now have something the world will never find anywhere else but at the feet of God and the throne of grace. It is real *peace*, and it begins by being at peace with God, the guaranteed result of justification.

With this kind of personal peace, there comes increasing levels of trust in God and respect for all of His other children. Our business dealings and work ethics will become known for fairness, honesty, and diligence. Our concern for the welfare of others will grow, as will our generosity. Most of all, this peace with God will last for eternity, because it depends on the resources and ability of our indwelling God and never on our fallen and sinful selves.

*** LOVE ***

Justification means I am at peace with God. Justification also means that I am truly loved by God! I know we are to love others as we do ourselves, but face it; we all need to be loved unconditionally, too. No life has meaning or value if that life is lived without receiving and giving love.

Usually when we speak of a great love in someone's life, we are thinking about a romantic love. In the Greek language there are three basic words for love, each defining a type of love. The first, *Eros*, refers to sexual, romantic love. The second word is *phileo* meaning love in the sense of fondness and friendship, of being a friend. *Phileo* is used in many compound constructions, such as *philarguria*, love of money, *philanthropia*, lover of mankind [philanthropist], and *philadelphia* is the Greek word for love of the brethren, or brotherly love. It is also the name of a city in Pennsylvania.

The third word for love in Greek is *agape*. It was not widely used as were *phileo* and *Eros*, so the New Testament authors 'shanghaied' *agape* and used it to distinguish and define Christian love in general, and God's love for us specifically. *Agape* is love that is unselfish and puts the needs of the one loved first. It does what is best for the one loved. I Corinthians 13 gives the best definition of *agape* love to be found. I am quoting verses 4-7, and 13:

"Love is patient, love is kind, and is not jealous; love does not brag and is not arrogant, does not act unbecomingly; it does not seek its own, is not provoked, does not take into account a wrong suffered, does not rejoice in unrighteousness, but rejoices with the truth; bears all things, believes all things, hopes all things, endures all things." "But now abide faith, hope, love, these three; but the greatest of these is love." This is the *agape* love we are to have for one another, but even more importantly; this is the love of a holy and perfect God for us, His imperfect children. Every Christian is truly and unconditionally loved in the best sense of the word!

What does God's *agape* love mean in practical, every day situations? Romans 8:26-39 describes *four* essential blessings which are vitally important to every justified believer. When God says "I love [*agape*] you," to a justified believer, this is what God means. [Please stop here and read Romans 8:26-39 before continuing!]

First of all, Romans 8:31 says, "If God is for us, who is against us?" The Greek structure of this sentence indicates the conditional "if" to mean, "If God is for us, *and He is*, then who is against us?" We need to remember that to achieve the status of being justified, while it is a gift to us, cost God the crucifixion of Christ. If God loved us in such a way that He was willing to sacrifice His Son for us, how could we ever believe that God will not continue to love us and protect us no matter what forces may hate and oppose us.

God and you are always the majority, no matter who or what is arraigned against you. God is and will always be on your side! He won't abandon any of us, not even when we mess up [which for some of us is frequent]. Psalm 118:6 says virtually the same thing: "The Lord is for me; I will not fear; What can man do to me?" The implied answer is absolutely nothing! In Christ we are finally and truly on the forever winning side.

Please note that Romans 8:31 started out saying "What then shall we say to these things?" "These things" refers to the context of the preceding five verses [Romans 8:26-30]. Some of the proof that God is for us begins with the intercession of the Holy Spirit in our prayers, insuring that we stay on track with the will of God. Moreover, no matter what seems to happen to us or even what we do, good or bad, God will cause it all to work together somehow, for our good and His.

Furthermore, there is a series of cause and effect events which God sets into motion for all those whom He will call "according to His purpose." [Romans 8:28b] God's call is based on His foreknowledge of each of us in particular, who He also predestined to become like Christ. He calls us, He justifies us, and He glorifies us. Although sanctification is not mentioned specifically, it is clearly alluded to in the process of conforming us "to the image of His Son [Rom. 8:29]." All of this is proof positive that God truly and unconditionally loves us!

The *second* blessing resulting from God's *agape* love for us is that God will provide everything we need. This was demonstrated by the fact that God did not even spare His own Son in order to save us [Rom. 8:32]. This does not mean, however, that God will give us everything we **want**. A love that always seeks another's best includes *not* spoiling them.

Probably the clearest way to understand how we need to respond to this blessing of God's love is found in the Sermon on the Mount. Beginning in Matthew 6:24, Jesus teaches us that no one can serve two masters. "You cannot serve God and Mammon." Mammon means riches, wealth or property, all secular signposts indicating 'success.' Here Jesus is explaining that we should not worry about acquiring the normal physical necessities of life, food, shelter and clothing. God knows we need these things and since God's love is also practical, His love is a promise to us that all these things will be provided.

Of course, God is also famous for frequently waiting until the last moment to make that provision. By doing it His way, He is also enlarging our faith and trust in Him. So when He says "do not be anxious" [Mt. 6:31], He does so because our anxiety belies a shortage of faith and trust. God understands our human frame, after all He did create us, and He knows what happened to us as a result of the fall. It is for good reason that our focus must always be kept on the God who supplies all of our needs, not on the needs themselves.

God sums up His lesson on faith, trust, and Divine providence in the last two verses of Matthew 6. "But seek first His kingdom, and His righteousness; and all these things shall be added to you. Therefore, do not be anxious for tomorrow; for tomorrow will care for itself. Each day has enough trouble of its own [How true!]." Of course, when you are laid off from work, your savings are all gone, and you have no idea how you will pay next month's rent or keep food on the table, it's understandably hard to *not* be **anxious**!

I have been there more than once, I was very anxious every time [my faith not being what it should have been and still isn't], and I wouldn't wish these circumstances on anyone. However, these kinds of situations do teach us how trustworthy God really is, and develop our faith for when we really are stuck in a crack. However, please remember when one is flat on their back the last thing they want or need is a lecture on faith.

James 2:15-17 says, "If a brother or sister [i.e. other Christians] is without clothing and in need of daily food, and one of you says to them, 'Go in peace, be warmed and be filled;' and yet you do not give them what is necessary for their body; what use is that? Even so faith, if it has no works, is dead, being by itself." If God directs us to demonstrate our faith in Him in tangible and practical ways, it is also reasonable to believe that He will practice what He preaches and demonstrate His love towards us in tangible and practical ways.

God also provides for all of our spiritual needs, because He wants us to stay focused on spiritual priorities. Ephesians 1:3 reads, "Blessed be the God and Father of our Lord Jesus Christ, who has blessed us with every spiritual blessing in the heavenly places in Christ." The rest of Ephesians, chapter one, basically identifies and explains all of our spiritual blessings, including a prayer for our ability to understand these things.

God also loves us enough to never let us take Him for granted. Living by faith is never easy; it is also never optional. It simply boils down to this; our satisfaction and happiness in life comes from maintaining our focus on God, on His love and our justification, on His plans and on His priorities.

The *third* blessing of God's love, is that God will always nullify all condemnation directed at us [Romans 8:33-34]. The Greek grammar indicates that this condemnation will be ongoing both now and on into the future. We must also recognize that *legalism* will be a major component of the condemnation we Christians will face, regardless of the source. Here again, is another excellent reason for being able to recognize legalism and reject it. The fact that we are fully justified before God through our Lord Jesus Christ, keeps on nullifying the criticism and condemnation we will repeatedly experience in this life.

There is only one source for our condemnation, but there are two distinct avenues from which our condemnation comes. The more obvious avenue is through other people. Family, friends, work associates, other Christians, and even strangers can condemn us for a variety of reasons, none of which are really important, but they are almost always very painful.

The other avenue, from which our condemnation comes, is from within. The criticism and condemnation from others can be almost nothing compared to the broken glass and burning coals over which we drag ourselves. Remember, nobody will ever be harder on you than *you*.

Working behind the scenes is the devil, the source of our condemnation. Nothing deflates an eager, enthusiastic Christian faster or better than criticism. Since we belong only to God forever, which Satan knows even if we don't, there is nothing Satan desires more than to keep us from ever learning this. Satan's success with the soul of a Christian is not in possessing it, since he can't, but rather in rendering that Christian ineffective and, for all intents and purposes, useless. Interestingly, military strategists have learned that wounding the enemy is actually more effective in winning a battle than killing them, because with the wounded you involve several other people in helping them, people who would otherwise be combatants themselves.

Condemnation should be a futile endeavor where Christians are concerned, because we have been justified by God's grace which springs from His agape love for us; God has nullified any and all condemnation directed at us forever! Romans 8:1 states unequivocally that "There is therefore now no condemnation for those who are in Christ Jesus."

The *final* blessing of God's *agape* love, found in Romans 8:35-39, is that God and I can never be separated. *Never!!* It is God's will that all who believe in Him, who have been justified by God's grace, be joined to Him for eternity. Nothing can ever separate us from God, once we become joined to Him through Christ Jesus. [cf. John 6:35-40]

However, I am sad to report that there are actually Christians who believe and teach that a Christian can lose their salvation. This is legalism at its worst, because it embraces a religious philosophy which places the burden for our salvation on us. If the burden of salvation is placed on you or me, no matter what the conditions we have to meet, aren't we in a very practical sense working to be saved? And wouldn't losing one's salvation mean being *separated* from God, and therefore

135

from His love? But didn't we just read that *absolutely nothing* can ever separate us from the love of God, which is in Christ Jesus? As Romans 9:16 says, "So then it does not depend on the man who wills [chooses] or the man who runs [works], but on God who has mercy."

*** ACCESS ***

A third benefit which results from our justification is not only the privilege but also the *right* to approach God in prayer any time we wish. After all, God *is* my Father, and we all know that a good Father will always take time to listen to His kids. Some of you may recall seeing a photograph of President John F. Kennedy conducting a meeting in the oval office. Right in the midst of all this important activity JFK's son is on his hands and knees playing under his dad's desk, while his dad smiles at him indulgently. I absolutely guarantee you if the Chairman of the Joint Chiefs of Staff tried that, the president would not be smiling! We are His children, and we are always welcome in his presence.

Of course, this does *not* mean the Father has to do whatever the children ask or desire of Him. Nevertheless, some people approach God and prayer as if they were giving orders to a waiter, or a heavenly bell-boy. God knows far better than we ever will, what is best for us. We need to remember this when the times come in which we want to vehemently disagree with Him. Our goal is to pray according to God's will, not according to our own agendas. Nevertheless, there is still nothing that can separate us from His love, not even our own anger, stupidity, or arrogance.

The Father's communication with us will be primarily through the Bible. If you really want to have a conversation with your heavenly Father, you will spend some of the time speaking to Him through prayer. The rest of the time you will need to listen to your Father, and the usual way that happens is through reading your Bible.

One of the ways to overcome any reticence or difficulty we have with prayer is to remember who we are talking to. Talking to royalty is quite different from speaking to one's father. I recall meeting an English lord a few years ago, and being a 'Colonial' not wishing to give offense, I had to ask someone [turned out to be his chauffeur] how to properly address him. I was told to address him as "your lordship," which I gratefully did, but I imagine his children just called him father, or dad. We don't want to be disrespectful when talking to God, but the King of heaven and earth does happen to be *our* Father Who loves us.

There are some interesting misconceptions about prayer and why we are instructed to pray. To begin with prayer is about *function*, not form. You can stand, sit, recline, jog, drive, and eat while praying. The important thing in prayer is that it is about *reality*.   When we pray for others, it must be about their *reality* and their known needs. The same goes for our personal prayers.

Another complication over prayer occurs when we reflect on the fact that our Father is the sovereign ruler of everything. If no thing and no one can resist doing what He says, and if He knows everything about everything, including our past, present, and future, then *why* do we ever have to ask for anything? God knows we are carbon-based life-forms, dependent on air, water, and groceries. That's the way He made us. So why are we told to pray for our daily bread?

We are told to pray because God *is* sovereign, and because we aren't. Prayer is not just a reminder to us of our constant need to rely on God's sovereign grace; *prayer **is** relying on God's sovereign grace*. Prayer is about practically depending completely on God in a specific situation, about specific needs. It is about our reality in real time!

***A CLEAR CONSCIENCE ***

A fourth benefit of our justification is a conscience cleansed of guilt. I Timothy 1:5 says that "…the goal of our instruction is love from a pure heart and a *good conscience*…" The Greek word used here for good is *agathos.* The other commonly used word for good is *kalos*. While *kalos* conveys the idea of good in the sense of beautiful or pleasing, *agathos* means good in the sense of fit, capable, and useful.

A good conscience in this context means one which is capable of loving [*agape*], a conscience sufficiently unfettered from trying to compensate for personal guilt, and freed of excess 'personal' baggage. It results in a person that is capable of serving others from *unselfish* motives. Ministry to others can be used in an attempt to make us feel better about ourselves or to make ourselves look better to others. This is a focal travesty we need to avoid.

Once sin is paid for, the guilt **must** be set aside. Laying aside our guilt is a *conscious mental exercise* based on Scripture. Not laying aside our guilt for sins Jesus paid in full for is denying that Christ's sacrifice on the cross is sufficient, and it is calling God a liar.

Setting aside the guilt associated with sins we commit before encountering Christ and salvation makes sense and is in most cases fairly easy to do. Setting aside the guilt over sins we commit after becoming believers is harder because we have already confessed our sins once and it feels somehow wrong to keep on sinning and confessing over and over. Sins that are particularly difficult to overcome, such as addictions and other deeply ingrained habits, make laying aside the guilt over these sins equally difficult.

As I said, setting aside our guilt is a mental exercise, but it must be solidly based on Scripture. The same goes for accepting forgiveness for *besetting* sins [sins that are hard to get rid of]. Alcoholics, drug addicts, people addicted to pornography, to gambling or to sex can have a terrible time trying to find a clean conscience.

For those of you who are wondering how many more times you will have to ask God's forgiveness for the same thing, I have some fairly good news. You can stop asking for forgiveness over and over because Christ died ONCE for all of your sins and all of mine, and all of the sins of every believer down to the end of time. And for anyone who is alive to read this, you must realize that when Christ died for your sins He did so some 2,000years ago!

Confession of sin is an entirely different matter, or should be. Confession and asking forgiveness over sin are two very different exercises, although they are obviously connected. We must always remember that the only sacrifice for sin is the death, burial, resurrection, and ascension of our Lord Jesus Christ.

If we continue to confess our sins in order to receive forgiveness for our sins, what we are doing, usually without realizing it, is trying to turn confession into a further sacrifice for sin. When repeated confession becomes a sacrifice for sin in our minds, we are actually though unintentionally denying the sufficiency of Christ's once for all sacrifice when He shed His blood on Calvary's cross.

The truth is that Christ has already paid for all of our sins, including the sins we keep committing repeatedly. If this is true, and it most certainly is, then why are we told to confess our sins whenever we commit them? The text on confessing sin most commonly referred to is I John 1:9, which certainly says that we must confess our sins in order to be cleansed of our unrighteousness. But is this verse talking about our *justification* or our *sanctification*?

The answer lies in a careful examination of the text and its' context. First, let us read this verse in a broader context and then examine the meaning of the word confess in the original tongue. I John1:8-11 says, "If we say we have no sin, we are deceiving ourselves, and the truth is not in us. If we confess our sins, He is faithful and righteous to forgive us our sins and to cleanse us from all unrighteousness. If we say that we have not sinned, we make Him a liar, and His word is not in us."

In this context, we first read "If we say we have no sin, we are deceiving ourselves. . ." Yet we have just begun understanding that because of the cross, we have been *justified* which means the penalty of sin has already been paid. If we are talking about our salvation in terms of our justification we can truthfully and correctly say "We have no sin, [because it has been paid for]." However, if we are talking about our sanctification then we are in the *process* of being delivered from the power of sin. In this context to say we have no sin, or have not sinned, would be grossly incorrect. I have been delivered from the penalty of sin, but I am still undergoing the process of being delivered from the power of sin. The point is at what aspect of our salvation is *confession* being discussed? From the context the obvious answer is that confession is a part of our sanctification process. Failure to confess sin in this context is not about losing or acquiring my salvation. It is about dealing with the guilt and damage to others that my sin is causing! It is ultimately about my spiritual growth.

The word "confess" in Greek is *homologeo* which literally means to *say the same thing*. When God confronts us with a sin in our lives, the thing He is seeking is to give us a better understanding and to agree [say the same thing] with God about this specific sin. At the same time we need to remember that it is only God and His strength and grace who is able to cleanse us from our unrighteousness. Confession is agreeing with God and again turning the problem over to God, no matter how many times we need to do it.

Many Christians are bothered by this idea that our responsibility is to turn the responsibility over to God. They feel that a Christian must make renewed and greater efforts to overcome their sins. But this is forgetting how and why we all got into trouble in the first place. Why do humans sin? Isn't our sin a result of original sin and our being born separated from God? If our separation from God causes our sin problem in the first place, how could our independent efforts ever repair and heal a sin problem? You can not save yourself. God must save you. Isn't that the point of grace? And isn't our only appropriate response faith? And isn't faith putting our trust in God and not relying on ourselves?

Many people struggling with alcohol or drug addictions participate in the Twelve Step Program developed by the founders of Alcoholics Anonymous. There are a great many addicts in recovery because of the success of taking these 12 steps. It is interesting that part of this successful process requires the addict to admit they are helpless, unable to overcome their addiction and need help. This is similar to the Christian's need to confess their sin and their helplessness to overcome sin in their own strength and to turn it over to God.

A parallel passage which helpfully illuminates the intent of John 1:8-10 is found in Psalms 32:1-5, particularly in verses 3-5! The first two verses of Psalms 32 are quoted in Romans 4:7-8 which is talking about our *justification*, while the next three verses in Psalms 32 are talking about our *sanctification*! Psalm 32:1-5 says, "How blessed is he whose transgression is forgiven, whose sin is covered! How blessed is the man to whom the Lord does not impute iniquity, and in whose spirit there is no deceit. When I kept silent about my sin [resisted confessing it], my body wasted away through my groaning all day long. For day and night Thy hand was heavy upon me [conviction]; My vitality was drained away as with the fever-heat of summer. I acknowledged my sin to Thee, and my iniquity I did not hide; I said I will confess my transgressions to the Lord; and thou didst forgive the **guilt** of my sin."

*** CONFIDENCE ***

Faith in Christ involves being assured of what He says He has done. Jesus says because He paid the price for our sins on the cross, we are now justified before God. Faith in Jesus is being convinced He will fully accomplish all His will in us and we will spend eternity being shown "the surpassing riches of His grace in kindness toward us in Christ Jesus [Ephesians 2:7]." And   Christian faith is relying on Christ to do what we must admit we can not do. Jesus is very clear about this as we can see in John 15:5, "I am the vine, you are the branches; he who abides in Me and I in him, bears much fruit; *for apart from Me you can do nothing.*"

For that matter, faith is really the only way to show our love for God. Words of worship may speak to us, but telling God we love Him in song and prayer will not mean anything if our actions do not try to speak as loudly as our words. If we want to tell God how much we love Him and how grateful we are for what He has done for us, then we need to *show* Him our love by *trusting* Him. Of course, before that we must first stop being afraid of Him.

Obviously, a life of faith demands *confidence* in God. At the same time confidence in God demands *faith*. Natural, fallen humanity is afraid of God because at some level we all know that we are guilty of sinning against God and deserve to be punished. There is no doubt this is what was motivating Adam and Eve when they hid from God in the Garden of Eden. Although sin is the problem, it is shame that prevents us from going to the only source that can solve our problem. We all want to be happy, but there is much unhappiness in life. Sin is the cause of our unhappiness whether we acknowledge it or not. This would be the first hurdle. Assuming we can admit that sin is the problem, our shame is still preventing us from going to the only source of healing. This would be the second hurdle. To get past this hurdle, we will have to trust that God will save us instead of condemning us, as we fear. But how will we find the confidence to actually trust God enough to come to Him to be saved? This would be the final and biggest hurdle.

II Corinthians 3:4 says, "And such *confidence* we have through Christ toward God." So Christ is the key, but how do we know this? Romans 10:17 says, "So faith comes from hearing, and hearing by the word of

Christ." We find the word of Christ in the Bible. But can we rely on the Bible to tell us the truth? Ephesians 2:8-9 says, "For by grace you have been saved by faith; and that not of yourselves, it is the gift of God; not as a result of works, that no one should boast."

Only God's infinite grace can provide us with the necessary confidence to trust Him to tell us the truth in the Bible and to save us. At the very heart of grace is the cross. But it is much more, beginning with the realization that grace and faith are a gift from God, not something that springs naturally from within man. It is because of the gift that we are able to start believing the Bible and learning not only what God wants from us, but even more importantly, what He has done for us and will do for us. Grace is the *only* way fallen man can get to God and stay there!

Having been given God's gift of grace which has enabled us to believe in the first place, now we start to learn what has happened to us and what will happen. One of the first lessons we must learn is the truth of justification, which means that the penalty and punishment issues are off the table *forever*! We didn't deserve justification, we didn't earn our justification, we couldn't even find justification; it had to find us through God's grace by faith. Knowing and believing the fact that we have been justified by grace + nothing helps us gain confidence in our Lord.

Justification is the key that lets you in the front door of the place where you now dwell with God your Father. Satan will not like having you believe this. The truth of our justification has been under attack since Christ dwelled among us and provided us with our justification. Justification has given us *confidence* in God through Christ. Justification has given us *a clear conscience*. A clear conscience is not about how we feel; it is what is true about us according to God. Justification has given us the right to *complete and constant access* to God. Don't listen to Satan when he tries to tell you otherwise, no matter how much of an 'angel of light' he may appear to be. Justification has given us the unlimited *love* of God. Don't say you are unworthy of this love; we already know that because it is same with the rest of us.

No human is worthy. In fact, it is not about us at all. It is about God who chose to love us before the foundation of the world and who decided to show us just how spectacular His grace really is. And as a result of all of this, because we have been justified, we now and forever after have *peace* with God. How blessed is God's assurance indeed? Amen!

***

"For I am confident of this very thing, that He who began a good work in you will perfect it until the day of Christ Jesus." Philippians 1:6

***

"It is God who is at work in you, both to will and to work for His good pleasure." Philippians 2:13

***

"Faithful is He who calls you, and He will also bring it to pass." I Thessalonians 5:24

***

"If we are faithless, He remains faithful; for He cannot deny Himself." II Timothy 2:13

***

"Do not be carried away by varied and strange teachings; for it is good for the heart to be strengthened by grace." Hebrews 13:9

***

"Now the God of peace, who brought up from the dead the great Shepherd of the sheep through the blood of the eternal covenant, even Jesus our Lord, equip you in every good thing to do His will, working in us that which is pleasing in His sight, through Jesus Christ; to whom be the glory forever and ever. Amen. Hebrews 13:20-21

***

Chapter Seven
BLESSED BROKENNESS

ANOTHER CONSEQUENCE OF GRACE

The purpose in breaking a wild mustang is not to break its spirit or irreparably harm it, but to *tame* it. The ultimate goal in breaking a wild mustang is to bend it's will sufficiently to it's owner's will to make the mustang useful to the one who owns and uses him and who is going to the trouble to break him. So it is with us. Because man is fallen, he is a "wild beast" by nature, and like our mustang, we all need to be broken and trained to be useful to our Master.

Being broken can be very unpleasant at times since being broken and being disciplined is essentially the same thing. As the writer of Hebrews reminds us, "All discipline for the moment seems not to be joyful, but sorrowful; yet to those who have been trained by it, afterwards it yields the peaceful fruit of righteousness. [Hebrews 12:11]

Brokenness is an unpopular doctrine with many middle class, upwardly mobile Christians because it conflicts so sharply with their expectations of a 'normal' Christian life. There are many who want to believe that by becoming a Christian they will not only insure their destination in the after life, they will also secure a relatively comfortable life in the present. After all they are constantly being told that God loves them and has a wonderful plan for their life. How could that include hardship or pain? But it does.

There is no doubt that being broken sounds unpleasant, and frequently it is. Consider the tone and the implications in these excerpts from a monograph entitled The Battle for Brokenness by Dan Edelen: "Real brokenness is the man who acknowledges that he is no longer his own; he has been bought with a price." "Here is the natural man broken by God. His pride is broken, his position is broken, his self-worship is broken. And in the place of all these comes praise to God for being broken by Him." "Dying to self means abandoning even our pain, no matter how great, to take on the image of the Savior." [20]

The truth is, the result of this breaking process yields blessed fruit in our lives that is not attainable by any other means. Consequently, instead of focusing on what we might lose, we could and should be focusing on what we are gaining. In any event, God is Sovereign, and He will always have His way, since His way is the *only* good and right way. But once in a while it is nice when He lets us catch a glimpse of what He is up to with us.

A good example of the results of brokenness involves our old friend, the relatively unknown Augustinian monk, who taught theology at the University of Wittenberg in Germany. This poor devil had some real problems with guilt, to the extent that he would frequently punish himself with a whip. Nevertheless, had it not been for God's plan for his life, we might never have heard of Martin Luther.

Because of his struggles with guilt, a mentor of Martin Luther finally convinced him to study his Bible more. As a result, Martin Luther discovered and came to understand the doctrine of true righteousness. Romans 1:17 made it so clear to Luther as he read, "But the righteous man shall live by faith." So it was the truth of Romans 1:17 that sparked the Protestant Reformation.

God had plans for Luther, which included being tormented with unrelenting feelings of guilt. But this torment also brought Martin Luther to a place where he could truly and deeply understand and grasp the wonderful fruit of being justified by grace through faith instead of by the efforts of the flesh. Martin Luther was cast into the role of becoming the leader of the Protestant Reformation, and he became probably the most influential Christian to live since the Apostles in the First Century. This is what I mean by '*blessed brokenness.*'

Paul the Apostle wrote about the problem we all have of relying on the flesh. The flesh refers to a human's natural wisdom, instincts and abilities apart from any connection to the Holy Spirit. Paul explains it this way in Philippians 3:2-11; "Beware of the dogs, beware of the evil workers, beware of the false circumcision; for we are the true circumcision, who worship in the Spirit of God and glory in Christ Jesus and put no confidence in the flesh, although I myself might have confidence even in the flesh. If anyone else has a mind to put confidence in the flesh, I far more: circumcised the eighth day, of the nation of Israel, of the tribe of Benjamin, a Hebrew of Hebrews; as to the Law, a Pharisee; as to zeal, a persecutor of the church; as to the righteousness which is in the Law, found blameless. But whatever things were gain to me, those things I have counted as loss for the sake of Christ. More than that, I count all things to be loss in view of the surpassing value of knowing Christ Jesus my Lord, for whom I have suffered the loss of all things, and count them but rubbish in order that I may gain Christ, and may be found in Him, not having a righteousness of my own derived from the Law, but that which is through faith in Christ, the righteousness which comes from God on the basis of faith, that I may know Him, and the power of his resurrection and the fellowship of His sufferings, being conformed to His death; in order that I may attain to the resurrection from the dead." *Every single Christian needs to know and understand what Paul is talking about in this passage! Every Christian needs to live like this.*

There are always those who misrepresent or even deny God's loving, sovereign grace. These false teachers and leaders will reject this principle of brokenness and its necessity, by either turning it into a *legalistic doctrine*, or by going so far as to reject brokenness as a *false doctrine*. None of us will ever learn from the Bible until we first learn to lay aside our own preconceived assumptions and expectations as well as everyone else's. Just because the Church, or your denomination has taught some particular view does not make it so **unless** it is what the Bible actually teaches!

If we reject a Biblical worldview, which includes the importance of brokenness and Divine discipline as *gifts* of God's grace, we are also incorrectly implying that we have some control over what happens to us based on our free wills and how much faith we have. Instead of being under grace, we are placing ourselves under a legalistic reward and punishment system which completely misuses, abuses, and ignores true faith. This, of course, brings us back around to all the frustration and sense of failure associated with legalism, trying to control our lives, and by our constant self-effort in trying to crank out an acceptable degree of faith.

THE HEALTH AND WEALTH 'GOSPEL'

Those who abide in a belief system that steadfastly maintains that the will of God is for every Christian to be healed and to remain healthy makes sickness a sin, proving the ill one's sinfulness and lack of faith. Along with the belief that physical health is an indicator of spiritual maturity, there is also the false belief that spiritual maturity results in financial success, making financial hardship another 'true' indicator of spiritual immaturity and a lack of faith.

The belief that the state of our health and wealth are directly tied to the amount of our faith or the spiritual maturity we possess is not only false, it is incredibly *cruel*. One can barely imagine the added sorrow and disillusionment for those who become seriously ill or handicapped as the results of an accident or disease and those who have suffered harsh financial reversals such as losing jobs or facing foreclosures on their homes. Whatever happened to those Christians who suffer with various handicaps and other hardships that are *according to the will of God*? We will soon meet such a man in this chapter. His name is Horatio Spafford.

Then there is the clear truth from God's word. The Apostle Peter wrote in I Peter 4:12-16, "Beloved, do not be surprised at the fiery ordeal among you, which comes upon you for your testing, as though some strange thing were happening to you; but to the degree that you share the sufferings of Christ, keep on rejoicing, so that also at the revelation of His glory you may rejoice with exultation. If you are reviled for the name of Christ, you are blessed, because the Spirit of glory and of God rests on you. Make sure that none of you suffers as a murderer, or thief, or evildoer, or a troublesome meddler; but if anyone suffers as a Christian, let him not feel ashamed, but in that name let him glorify God."

The greatest tragedy to befall a Christian are not the illnesses and losses we may have to endure, but the criticism and condemnation of other Christians that believe and teach that we are second class Christians getting what we deserve. And this is nothing compared to the criticism and condemnation we end up heaping upon ourselves if we believe these false doctrines.

We have either forgotten or never knew to begin with, that God's grace is not a free pass to avoid hardship and disappointment. The truth is that grace is the **only** protection we have when we must face the hard experiences that cause spiritual growth. In the great and profound hymn, Amazing Grace, John Newton wrote these words:

> *Through many dangers, toils, and snares,*
> *I have already come;*
> *Tis grace hath brought me safe thus far,*
> *And grace will lead me home.*[21]

"Dangers, toils, and snares" are a much better and more accurate description of the normal Christian life than are good health and a Mercedes in the garage. Ray Stedman, a well-known Bible teacher, pastor, and author, once described a normal Christian as someone who was always praising God, and *always in trouble*.

THE INCREDIBLE TESTIMONY OF HORATIO and ANNA SPAFFORD

Not every tragedy that befalls us is a disciplinary action from God, nor does it occur just to break us. Indeed, I think real tragedies often happen to Christians who already have some brokenness and are having a closer walk with God. Their ability to survive various trials and temptations and emerge victorious in Christ with an even closer walk with the Lord is another glowing testimony to the grace and faithfulness of our God.

For a few Christians, the things they must face can be incredibly difficult. Anyone who has experienced the kinds of tragedies that befell Horatio and Anna Spafford, and then seen the outcome of their lives, can only be awed by the grace of God that led them and sustained them.

In light of their tragedies, what would Horatio and Anna have done if they believed these things happened to them because of their lack of faith? And how would they be viewed and treated by those who believe tragedy is a result of sinfulness and/or faithlessness?

It Is Well with My Soul is a truly great hymn with an even greater story behind the writing of it. The lyrics to this great hymn were written by our hero, Horatio G. Spafford, in 1873. The music for this hymn was written by Philip P. Bliss in 1876, which he also entitled <u>Ville du Havre</u>, the name of an important French steamship.

The name of Horatio Spafford is not well known to most of us in this century, but it was very familiar to the citizens of Chicago, Illinois in the 1860's. Mr. Spafford was a wealthy Chicago lawyer and developer, a well-known and respected Christian, and a prominent supporter and close friend of the great evangelist, Dwight L. Moody. That it was 'well with the soul' of a wealthy, successful, happily married family man would not seem particularly remarkable, but as we shall see, his fortunes were about to change. It is important to remember that the words of this great hymn were written **after** *three* crushing tragedies struck the Spafford family in a span of less than four years.

The first tragedy occurred in 1870, when the Spafford's only son died from scarlet fever. He was just four years old. Children are supposed to outlive their parents, not the other way around. So one would think this is enough of a burden to bear, but he would be wrong.

One year later, Horatio, who had invested heavily in real estate along the shores of Lake Michigan, had every one of his properties destroyed in the great Chicago fire of 1871. First, they lost their son, and then they were ruined financially. This would seem like *more* than enough to bear, but again we would be wrong, for there was still more to come.

Two years later, in 1873, Dwight Moody was conducting an evangelistic campaign in Britain and had requested Horatio Spafford's help. Aware of the emotional toll the two tragedies had taken on his family, Horatio decided to take his wife and four daughters along for a holiday while he worked with Moody.

They planned to join Dwight Moody in England in late 1873. The family traveled to New York where they were to take passage on the French steamer <u>Ville du Havre</u>. At the last minute before they set sail, Mr. Spafford was forced to delay due to some pressing business. Not wanting to ruin the family's holiday, Horatio persuaded his wife and daughters to go ahead as planned while he returned to Chicago. He would rejoin them as quickly as possible.

Nine days later Spafford received a telegram from his wife who had reached Wales. It simply said "Saved alone." It seems that on November 22, 1873 the <u>Ville du Havre</u> collided with an English vessel, the <u>Lochearn</u>. The <u>Ville du Havre</u> sank in only twelve minutes, claiming the lives of 226 souls. Anna Spafford, clinging tightly to her four daughters Annie, Maggie, Bessie, and Tanetta, stayed together on the deck until the force of the sea swept them all away. Anna alone was spared when a wooden plank from the ship floated up beneath her unconscious body and supported her until help arrived. Their four precious daughters all perished.

Upon receiving the heart breaking news, Horatio took passage on the next ship crossing the Atlantic, to join his devastated wife. The Captain of this ship summoned Horatio to the bridge and told him that according to their best calculations they were just passing over the point where the <u>Ville du Havre</u> sank. The sea there, he was told, was three miles deep.

Returning to his cabin, Horatio penned the following lyrics of this great hymn. Please think about what you are reading, against this tragic background, carefully and thoughtfully:

IT IS WELL WITH MY SOUL
When peace, like a river, attendeth my way,
When sorrows like sea billows roll;
Whatever my lot, Thou has taught me to say,
It is well, it is well, with my soul.
Refrain
It is well, with my soul,
It is well, with my soul,
It is well, it is well, with my soul.

Though Satan should buffet, though trials should come,
Let this blest assurance control,
That Christ has regarded my helpless estate,
And hath shed His own blood for my soul.
Refrain
My sin, oh, the bliss of this glorious thought!

My sin, not in part but the whole,
Is nailed to the cross, and I bear it no more,
Praise the Lord, praise the Lord, O my soul!
Refrain
For me, be it Christ, be it Christ hence to live:
If Jordan above me shall roll,
No pang shall be mine, for in death as in life
Thou wilt whisper Thy peace to my soul.
Refrain
But, Lord, 'tis for Thee, for Thy coming we wait,
The sky, not the grave, is our goal;
Oh trump of the angel! Oh voice of the Lord!
Blessed hope, blessed rest of my soul!
Refrain
And Lord, haste the day when my faith shall be sight,
The clouds be rolled back as a scroll;
The trump shall resound, and the Lord shall descend,
Even so, it is well with my soul.
Refrain

THE GREAT FALSE ASSUMPTION

Why do *bad* things like sickness, poverty, and even death happen to *good* people? If we are to follow the 'logic' of the health and wealth 'gospel', bad things *can't* happen to good people, that is, *people of faith*. Bad things only happen to people who are weak or lacking in faith. If this were true, then how do we explain the tragic experiences of Horatio and Anna Spafford?

By the way, this goofy kind of reasoning doesn't just belong to the health and wealth advocates. This distorted way of thinking reflects the natural tendency of all mankind to take for granted that life's events, both good and bad, are somehow a result of one's *karma* or behavior.

Here again we see the results of Adam and Eve's disobedience [the original sin]. Mankind, filled with the 'knowledge' of good and evil, always wants to think we are basically good and in control. Building on this assumption, fallen man's idea of justification is that it is a *reward* for his good works and efforts. If we are sufficiently good, which means we do more good than evil, then we deserve 'justification' or approval/ salvation.

This is the *Great False Assumption*; that mankind is *basically good*. Yet the Bible tells us that every one of us is sinful by nature, guilty before God, and sentenced to death. So then how in the world could any of us be considered '*good?*'

Luke 18:18-23 relates a conversation between Jesus and a rich young ruler who wanted to be told he was good enough to go to heaven. So this young rich ruler questioned Jesus, saying, "Good Teacher, what shall I do to obtain eternal life?' And instead of an immediate answer, Jesus asked him a totally unexpected question: "Why do you call Me good? No one is good except God alone [Luke 18:18-19]."

Then Jesus went on to mention five of the Ten Commandments. Now the young ruler thinks he is on firm ground and he tells Jesus that he has kept the commandments from his youth.

However, instead of receiving Christ's approval and admiration [which he was obviously expecting], Jesus told him he still lacked one thing; liquidate all your wealth and give it to the poor. Then Jesus told him that if he does this he will have treasure in heaven, and so he is to take up following Jesus. Instead, the rich young ruler "... when he heard these things, he became very sad; for he was extremely rich."

The truth is that mankind is completely lost, dead in their sins and trespasses, and all of humanity has been ever since Adam. Our Lord's statements to this arrogant and rich young ruler were designed to rid him of the false notion that there was anything good in him. There is nothing good in humanity for which we can take credit or by which we can obtain salvation. It just *can't* happen!!

The correct answer was and is that only God Himself is *good!* Since the rich young ruler had addressed Jesus as "good Teacher" he first had to learn that Jesus was and is *divine*. Any theological system that bases any of its teachings on human merit is completely and disastrously *wrong* as is anyone who attempts to diminish in any way the absolute sovereignty of our Lord!

The correct question to ask is why do *good* things ever happen to *bad* people? The correct answer is because of God's *grace!* Fortunately, for all of us who are protected by God's *grace, no believer gets what we actually deserve in eternity*. This is the true gospel and the absolute wonder of God's eternal *grace*.

ALLS WELL THAT ENDS WELL

The following was written about the character and conduct of Horatio and Anna that "Spafford and his wife had a consistent history of acting on their faith. After the great Chicago fire 0f 1871, they devoted countless hours to helping the survivors. In 1881, they moved to Jerusalem (taking two daughters born after the shipwreck tragedy) and helped found a group called the American Colony; its mission was to serve the poor."[22] Horatio Spafford died from malaria October 16, 1888, four days before his sixtieth birthday. He is buried in Jerusalem, Israel.

We would be wise to ask what it is about God's *grace* that enabled Horatio and Anna Spafford to survive and endure such tragedy and to keep on worshipping and serving God. Their knowledge of God's grace worked for them the same as it will for us. Look again at Horatio's hymn. The recurrent theme in the face of all that happened, the easy and the hard, is that we the unworthy and undeserving have been saved from our sin by the shed blood of Christ, and that having been fully *justified* at the cross, we are assured of our eternal salvation and final glorification in Christ, *no matter what*. It was well with Horatio's soul because of Who he believed in and that what the Bible said had to be true.

Obviously, Horatio and Anna's well-being *never* depended on how they felt or what they had to go through. After all, they had to have felt completely devastated and even abandoned, far beyond anything most of us could even imagine. Nevertheless, our *feelings* can never change the truth!

By the way, there is a sadly ironic footnote to this story. Philip P. Bliss, who wrote the music for It Is Well With My Soul along with many other hymns, and his wife died in a fiery train wreck in 1876, shortly after writing the music for It Is Well With My Soul.

Here is another thought; perhaps death for a Christian is a privilege and a reward, not a tragedy or a punishment. However, to believe this we need a much better handle on brokenness and true grace. So beware the delusional, legalistic, health and wealth, name it and claim it, man is basically good or should be *crowd*.

ON FIRE FOR GOD

Those who deny the process of being broken, let alone our need for real brokenness, erect another significant *obstacle to grace* in many Christian's lives. Concerning this process of brokenness, perhaps we should review again what the Word of God has to say to us about discipline and brokenness.

It is written in I Peter 4:12-13 and 19; "Beloved, do not be surprised at the fiery ordeal among you, which comes upon you for your testing, as though some strange thing were happening to you; but to the degree that you share the sufferings of Christ, keep on rejoicing; so that also at the revelation of His glory, you may rejoice with exultation. . . . Therefore, let those also who suffer according to the will of God entrust their souls to a faithful Creator in doing what is right." Here is the plain simple Biblical truth: There *will* be fiery ordeals for our testing, we *will* share the sufferings of Christ, and our suffering *will be according to the will of God*.

One example of the breaking process many of us are familiar with is a difficult period in our lives that was instrumental in bringing us to faith in Christ. Looking at a "fiery ordeal" in this light, we can easily look back on it and honestly praise God for it. Even though it was painful to go through at the time, the result was our salvation, and there is nothing better or greater that can happen to us than being eternally saved in Christ by God's grace!

There are other passages of Scripture, which refer to the importance about brokenness. Peter begins his first epistle with the following truths [which are inseparably connected]; "Blessed be the God and Father of our Lord Jesus Christ, who according to His great mercy has caused us to be born again to a living hope through the resurrection of Jesus Christ from the dead, to obtain an inheritance which is imperishable and undefiled and will not fade away, reserved in heaven for you, who are protected by the power of God through faith for a salvation ready to be revealed in the last time. In this you greatly rejoice, even though now for a little while, if necessary, you have been distressed by various trials [or temptations], that the proof of your faith, being more precious than gold which is perishable, even though tested by fire, may be found to result in praise and glory and honor at the revelation of Jesus Christ." [I Peter 1:3-7]

Testing gold with fire meant melting the gold. This in turn would cause any impurities in the gold to come to the surface. Then the impurities could be skimmed 0ff, making the gold, now tested, that much more valuable. A faith tested by fiery ordeals is a faith that is having the impurities removed by the testing and becoming that much more valuable.

This is why James writes, "Consider it all joy, my brethren, when you encounter various trials [or temptations]; knowing that the testing of your faith produces endurance [or steadfastness]. And let endurance have its perfect result [or work], that you may be perfect [or mature] and complete, lacking in nothing." [James 1:2-4]

Look also at what Paul has to say about trials in Romans 5:3-5: "And not only this, but we also exult in our tribulations [or troubles]; knowing that tribulation [or trouble] brings about perseverance; and perseverance, proven character; and proven character, hope; and hope does not disappoint; because the love of God has been poured out within our hearts through the Holy Spirit who was given to us."

The word "tribulation" or "trouble" which is used twice in the Romans passage just quoted is translated from the Greek *thlipsis,* a word that literally means "pressing" or "pressure." In the Bible, *thlipsis* is always used metaphorically, but the idea in tribulation or affliction is something that is causing us physical and mental or emotional stress or pressure. And the Bible says this stressful pressure is a very good thing for us to experience.

AN UNUSUAL METAPHOR

There is a reproduction of a painting on the wall of our family room, which depicts Jesus as a shepherd carrying a lamb on His shoulders. There is a story behind this picture. It seems that in ancient times shepherds had a method for curing wayward sheep of this tendency to keep wandering off. Using his staff, the shepherd would break one of the sheep's legs. Then he would carry the animal around on his shoulders [like Jesus in the painting] until the broken leg healed. The result of this bizarre method was that the wandering sheep wandered no more, but stayed very close to the shepherd for the rest of his life.

I do not recall where I first heard this story, and I do not even know for sure if it is true but I hope it is. However, whether human shepherds ever used this method on actual sheep or not, what I *do* know for sure is that God *does* use this method. God breaks legs. Usually, as we will soon see from Scripture, the 'broken leg' is metaphorical, not literal.

Nevertheless, I know personally of at least one instance when God did literally break the ankle of a wandering lamb. This particular lamb was also destined to later become my wife, and along with the honeymoon and the new joys of marriage, I also got to pay Judy's medical bills for her broken ankle.

"YOU FOLLOW ME!"

In the last chapter of the Gospel according to John, the disciple and soon to be Apostle Peter once again got his foot stuck in his mouth. In John21:20-22 we read, "Peter, turning around, saw the disciple whom Jesus loved following them; the one who also had leaned back on His breast at the supper, and said 'Lord, who is the one who betrays You?' Peter therefore seeing him said to Jesus, 'Lord, and what about this man?' Jesus said to him, 'If I want him to remain until I come, what is that to you? *You follow Me!*'"[23]

One of the reasons God has for "breaking our legs," is to get us to stay close to Jesus and His flock, and to follow Him carefully. Since we believers in Christ are referred to as the sheep of His flock, and Jesus is the chief shepherd, the analogy of the shepherds breaking the legs of wandering sheep may just be true. In any event, God's *discipline* is always for our greater good, and will always aim at making us better at following and relying on his grace, even if it hurts a little at the time.

"YOU REVEAL ME"

In II Corinthians 4: 7, we are told this; "But we have this treasure in earthen vessels, that the surpassing greatness of the power may be of God and not from ourselves." Now this "treasure" we have is our Lord Jesus. The "earthen vessels" refer to us. If we can imagine a clay pot filled with pieces of gold, silver, and gems, then we have a good picture of our *primary purpose* in life.

Humans without Christ indwelling them are empty, useless clay pots. Look inside the pot, and you will see nothing. However, when God places the priceless treasure of His *life* in us, through what we call salvation or receiving Christ, then we Christians become *living treasure chests*. Now that we realize how rich we have become by God's grace, we need to think about what we are to do with this treasure. How indeed will He want to spend it?

The Sermon on the Mount is found in Matthew, chapter 5. Please note the two metaphors Jesus uses to describe our basic function or ministry in life, as those filled with divine treasures. Jesus said to us, "You are the salt of the earth; but if the salt has become tasteless, how will it be made salty again? It is good for nothing anymore, except to be thrown out and trampled under foot by men. You are the light of the world. A city set on a hill cannot be hidden. Nor do men light a lamp, and put it under the peckmeasure, but on the lampstand; and it gives light to all who are in the house. Let your light shine before men in such a way that they may see your good works, and glorify your Father who is in heaven." [Matthew 5: 13-16]

We are most familiar with salt as a common and inexpensive food seasoning. However, salt has an impressive history. There are currently over 14,000 uses for salt, or sodium chloride. Wikipedia, the free online encyclopedia, says this about salt; "Salt's preservative ability was a foundation of civilization. It eliminated dependency on the seasonal availability of food and allowed travel over long distances. . . . However, salt was difficult to obtain, and so it was a highly valued trade item. Until the 1900s, salt was one of the prime movers of national economies and wars. Salt was taxed as far back as the 20th century BC in China.[24]

"It is believed that Roman soldiers were at certain times paid with salt, and this is still evident in the English language, as the word "salary" is derived from the Latin word *salarium* that means payment in salt ... It [salt] was also of high value to the Hebrews, Greeks and other peoples of antiquity." Salt was exported, transported and taxed to the extent that it "... has played a prominent role in determining the power and location of the world's great cities. Salt created and destroyed empires... Cities, states and duchies along the salt roads extracted heavy duties and taxes for the salt passing through their territories. This practice even caused the formation of cities, such as the city of Munich in 1158 . . . The *gabelle* - a hated French salt tax - was enacted in 1286 and maintained until 1790." Because of these taxes . . . common salt was of such a high value that it caused mass population shifts and exodus, attracted invaders and caused wars."[25]

The simple reason salt was so valuable was that it provided the only way to preserve meat and fish for long periods up until the invention of mechanical refrigeration. When Jesus was delivering the Sermon on the Mount, those listening understood clearly that salt was a valuable and fundamental necessity to the foundation of civilization. In other words, Jesus wants us to realize not only our extreme value in the course of human affairs, but also the importance of our undergirding of civilization, tasks of infinitely more importance than preserving foods with salt.

Along with being 'treasure chests' and 'salt', Jesus also told us we are the light of the world. He said a "city set upon a hill cannot be hidden." Our Lord further clarified what He was driving at by pointing out that no one lit a lamp only to then conceal it. As a brief side note, most lamps of this period were made of clay and burned oil, which is a common biblical metaphor for the Holy Spirit. So we are chests full of treasure, salt for the preserving of that which is otherwise going to spoil and hopefully unconcealed sources of light for everyone in the world so that no one needs to stumble in the darkness.

The final point Jesus makes is that we Christians are to conduct our ministry activity in such a way so that those who are paying any attention at all, will see that what we are saying and doing *reveals the indwelling presence of the Lord our God*. Now, in order for the world to *see* our Holy *source*, we are going to have to be spilled, lit up on fire, and thoroughly broken. Revealing or manifesting Jesus means making Him [not us] visible to the universe. Best way to do that, I am sorry to say, is to break the pot so everyone can see what is inside! This is what is meant by brokenness, and this is why it is so important.

BREAK A LEG

Brokenness before God and the world is a process by which each Christian, to whatever extent God has determined, are intended to lose their importance and significance in their own eyes and in the eyes of those around them and who know them. Jesus had returned to His hometown of Nazareth briefly, and was teaching in the synagogue. Matthew 13:57 says that His reception among them was less than enthusiastic. We read, "And they took offense at Him. But Jesus said to them, 'A prophet is not without honor except in his home town, and in his own household.'"

When the world looks at us, God wants them to see Jesus. Meanwhile, many of us are busy trying to keep a low profile or, as they say, to "stay below the radar" because we don't want to be singled out as 'one of those Christians/Jesus freaks/religious nuts/etc.' Very simply put, we are a little embarrassed to be identified as one of His followers, primarily because we do not think we are very good representatives. This problem stems from a deluge of bad doctrine which says we have to be exemplary representatives of God, ready to witness at a moments notice. Only if we are near perfect replications of Christ will the world see and turn to Christ for salvation. This certainly does not sound like *more of Him and less of me*!

There is another group that is constantly trying to draw attention to themselves in hopes the world will see how truly spiritual they are. In Jesus' time they were called the Pharisees, and in every age there will always be legalistic, self-righteous 'Christians' strutting around some-where. Of course, it is a good bet that at least some, if not all, of these folks are propelled by a variety of psychological maladies. By the way, we would do well to remember that our Lord did not have any kind words for Pharisees. Neither hiding nor strutting will accomplish what God wants, which is to reveal Jesus to our contemporary world, so it is probably safe to say that *breaking* will continue at least until the rapture.

A little further on in the Sermon on the Mount Jesus addressed these two problems of ours, hiding or strutting, by teaching, "Do not lay up for yourselves treasures upon earth, where moth and rust destroy, where thieves break in and steal, but lay up for yourselves treasures in heaven, where neither moth or rust destroys, and where thieves do not break in or steal; for where your treasure is, there will your heart be also. . . . No one can serve two masters; for either he will hate the one and love the other, or he will hold to one and despise the other. You cannot serve God and Mammon [or riches]. . . . Do not be anxious then, saying 'What shall we eat?' or, 'What shall we drink?' or, 'With what will we clothe ourselves?' For all these things the Gentiles eagerly seek; for your heavenly Father knows that you need all these things. But seek first His kingdom and His righteousness; and all these things shall be added [or provided] to you. Therefore do not be anxious for tomorrow; for tomorrow will take care of itself. Each day has enough trouble of its own." [Matthew 6:19-21, 24, 31-34] Easy to say, hard to do! This is WHY God enables and equips us to do what He wishes, in part by 'breaking our legs.'

II Corinthians 4 has a lot to say on this important subject of brokenness, so we are going to spend some time in it. However, lets begin by turning briefly to II Corinthians 3:4-6, where we read, "And such confidence we have through Christ toward God. Not that we are adequate in our selves to consider anything as coming from ourselves, but our adequacy is from God, who also made us servants of a new covenant, not of the letter, but of the Spirit; for the letter [of the Law] kills, but the Spirit gives life."

The context is ministry to others and how it will be accomplished. The first thing we should note is our own *personal inadequacy*. What God wants, we cannot supply or achieve, but God *will* equip and enable us to do exactly what He wants, when He wants it, and in the way He wants it done. Consequently, II Corinthians 4:1 begins with these words; "Therefore, since we have this ministry, as we received mercy, we do not lose heart." Two important things to remember; brokenness is about our ministry to others, and do not get discouraged by the problems we encounter along the way because they are helping to accomplish brokenness in us.

II Corinthians 4:7 alerts us to the fact that we have what the world **needs**, whether they realize it or not, or we realize it or not, and this treasure [Christ] comes to them in earthen vessels [us], ". . . that the surpassing greatness of the power may be of God and not from ourselves."

What now follows in II Corinthians 4:8-9 pretty much defines what 'breaking' is going to be like and what we can expect as a normal feature of our Christian walk; "we are *afflicted* in every way, but not crushed; *perplexed*, but not despairing; *persecuted*, but not forsaken; *struck down*, but not destroyed." We needn't complain either, for these experiences happen to everyone. However, only the Christians really benefit from them!

There are four basic ways God goes about 'breaking our legs.' The first is through *afflictions*. This refers to **external pressures** [which is the normal cause of broken legs]. The Greek word is *thlibo* meaning to compress, restrict, confine, oppress. We will all face a lot of external pressures, or stress. Illness, injury, loss of jobs, lack of financial resources, loss of loved ones, disappointments, failures, even divorces and imprisonment, all those things that press in on us, distract us, and even cause us to doubt God at times. But for all the pressure or stress we may be subjected to, God has promised that *we will never be crushed!*

The second method God uses to 'break a leg', is to *perplex* us. The Greek word used here is *aporeo*, which means to be at a loss as to what to do, to be in doubt, uncertain, and anxious. This is an **inner pressure**, a mental or moral stress that may or may not be the result of external pressures, but it would also go hand in hand with external pressures. You lose your job and your ability to work in the field of your experience and expertise, and now you don't know what to do or where to go. You would be perplexed, not to mention stressed, but again God has promised that *we would not become despairing*. This Greek word, *eksaporeo*, is a more intensive form of the word for perplexes, *aporeo*, and means to be in great difficulty, doubt, embarrassment, even to despair of living.

This doesn't mean we won't have moments that seem overwhelming. After all, the point of brokenness, or being broken, is to take us way beyond our human or natural abilities and limitations, so that we have to learn to rely only on God, knowing that if He doesn't come through, neither will we! This can be very scary sometimes, but God has promised to always be with us. Once you become an elderly Christian, having walked with the Lord for *many* years, you start to understand His promises really are true because you have experienced the truth of His promises for yourself repeatedly. But I will always wonder why experience and wisdom weren't reserved for the young who would seem to have the energy to use it and benefit from it!

The third method God uses to 'break a leg,' is **persecution**. The Greek word is *dioko*, which not only means to persecute, but to pursue after something, or be pursued, to drive away or drive out, to seek after diligently, strive for, even aspire to. Paul uses this word in a positive sense in Philippians 3:14 where it is translated "press on," to describe Paul's pursuit ". . . toward the goal for the prize of the upward call of God in Christ Jesus."

We should remember that persecution isn't just the angry attitude of unbelievers towards Christians, but more importantly, it refers to *the opposition of Satan against all Christians*, and his attempts to discredit, demotivate, and disillusion us. The devil is constantly seeking someone to "devour" and he will surely manage to take a bite out of us from time to time. These can be very humbling times in a Christian's life. But Satan will never win or prevail against us, because God promises never to abandon us.[26]

The fourth method God uses to 'break a leg' is for us to be **struck down**. This is just what the Greek word *kataballo* means, to throw down or strike down. Horatio and Anna Spafford were certainly struck down and more than once. But God promised never to destroy them and they weren't!

Of course, one might ask about the destruction of their son from scarlet fever, and their four daughters who perished in the sinking of the "Ville du Havre." This word *destroy* in Greek is *apollumi*. It means to ruin, destroy, kill, put to death in the sense of ETERNAL DESTRUCTION or ETERNAL DEATH, which is the fate only of the non-believer. Horatio Spafford died on October 16, 1888. Be assured his children were waiting on that wonderful day to welcome him home!

Psalm 116:15 says "Precious in the sight of the Lord is the death of his Godly ones." The Godly ones are all who have been declared righteous by grace through faith, and the children of the righteous are sanctified by their parent's faith.

Brokenness, however it may come, is *never* a punishment. Like discipline, it is a gift of God's grace, because brokenness is what allows us and helps us to be conformed to the image of Christ. Hebrews 12:11

reminds us that "All discipline for the moment seems not to be joyful, but sorrowful; yet to those who have been trained by it, afterwards it yields the peaceful fruit of righteousness."

We may be affected physically, emotionally, or intellectually. Sometimes the breaking process is directed at our minds, sometimes at our bodies, but however we encounter the Lord, we will always encounter spiritual growth and blessing. And speaking of blessings, take a few moments now to read all the way through Romans 8:26-38!

THE BLESSINGS OF BROKENNESS

In II Corinthians 4, immediately following the four areas or ways which explain *how* we are being broken, comes an in depth explanation about *why* we are being broken. The Apostle Paul continues, ". . . always carrying about in the body [our body] the dying of Jesus, that the life of Jesus also may be manifested in our body. For we who live are constantly being delivered over to death for Jesus' sake, that the life of Jesus also may be manifested in our mortal flesh. So death works in us, but life in you." [II Corinthians 4:10-12]

Jesus emphatically states a *spiritual principle* in John 12:24, which will not change nor be modified because we might not like the way it sounds. It is this: "Truly, truly, I say to you,[27] unless a grain of wheat falls into the earth and dies, it remains by itself alone; but if it dies, it bears much fruit." This analogy applies, first of all, to the death, burial, and resurrection of our Lord Jesus Christ. In other words, it was absolutely imperative that Jesus be crucified, buried, and resurrected. The fruit born of His death and resurrection is you and me, and every other born-again believer who has ever existed.

This *principle* is repeated in every Christian's life. First of all, it is the means of our own salvation. It is how salvation actually works. Paul describes and applies this mechanism in Romans 6:2-11: "...How shall we who died to sin still live in it? Or do you not know that all of us who have been baptized into Christ Jesus have been baptized into His death? Therefore we have been buried with Him through baptism into death, in order that as Christ was raised from the dead through the glory of the Father, so we too might walk in newness of life. For if we have become united with Him in the likeness of His death, certainly we shall be also in the likeness of His resurrection, knowing this, that our old self [or man] was crucified with Him, that our body of sin might be done away with, [or rendered powerless] that we should no longer be slaves to sin; for he who has died is freed [or acquitted] from sin. Now if we have died with Christ, we believe that we shall also live with Him, knowing that Christ, having been raised from the dead, is never to die again; death no longer is master over Him. For the death that He died, He died to sin, once for all; but the life that He lives, He lives to God. Even so consider yourselves to be dead to sin, but alive to God in Christ Jesus."

Paul again refers to the *principle* while explaining the resurrection of the dead. He writes in I Corinthians 15:35-36 and 42-44a, "But someone will say, 'How are the dead raised? And with what kind of body do they come?' You fool! That which you sow does not come to life unless it dies;" ... "So also is the resurrection of the dead. It is sown a perishable body, it is raised an imperishable body; it is sown in dishonor, it is raised in glory; it is sown in weakness, it is raised in power; it is sown a natural body, it is raised a spiritual body."

This is the same *principle* at work in II Corinthians 4. First, compare verse 10 with the passage just quoted from Romans 6. We are continually and eternally associated with Christ's death and resurrection. Should we forget this *principle,* it will in no way prevent this *principle* from working. II Corinthians 4:11-12 says, "For we who live are constantly being delivered over to death for Jesus' sake, that the life of Jesus also may be manifested in our mortal flesh. So death works in us, but life in you." This is how we will grow spiritually, and this is how we will be able to minister to others spiritually! There is no other way.

What are the blessings? Well, first, we are to live *resurrected lives,* or we might say we are to live on the *resurrection* side of life. We are to live in *victory*, not defeat. This doesn't mean victory is painless, and what we may define as victory or defeat may be defined and viewed quite differently by God.

This *resurrected life* is also an *exchanged* life. Paul explained it this way; "I have been crucified with Christ; and it is no longer I who live, but Christ lives in me; and the life which I now live in the flesh I live by faith in the Son of God, who loved me and delivered Himself up for me." (Galatians 2:20)

I will not always live faithfully and trustingly, after all, I am still mortal. But not to worry, God *will* keep on delivering me [and you] over to death by affliction, perplexity, persecution, and tragedy so that our lives will have to manifest the life of Christ.

The *resurrected* or *exchanged* life can also be described as the *abiding* life. Jesus taught us in John 15:4-5, "Abide in Me, and I in you. As the branch cannot bear fruit of itself, unless it abides in the vine, so neither can you, unless you abide in Me. I am the vine, you are the branches; he who abides in Me, and I in him, he bears much fruit; for apart from Me you can do nothing." This does not mean we cannot or will not be active. It just means we will not do any good unless and until we are doing something that originates in the mind and heart of God, and is operating according to His strength and power, not ours. We will never ever be able to crank out anything even remotely close to authentic spirituality by ourselves.

How great is the *resurrected, exchanged, abiding* life? Consider Galatians 5: "But the fruit of the Spirit is love, joy, peace, patience, kindness, goodness faithfulness, gentleness, self-control; against such things there is no law. Now those who belong to Christ Jesus have crucified the flesh with its passions and desires. If we live by the Spirit, let us also walk by the Spirit [or follow the Spirit]." (Galatians 5:22-25) There is a great poem written by the late Dr. A. B. Simpson. You may already be familiar with it but it still bears repeating in this context.

HIMSELF

Once it was the blessing, now it is the Lord;
Once it was the feeling, now it is His Word;
Once His gifts I wanted, now the Giver own;
Once I sought for healing, now Himself alone.

Once 'twas painful trying, now 'tis perfect trust;
Once a half salvation, now the uttermost;
Once 'twas ceaseless holding, now He holds me fast
Once 'twas constant drifting, now my anchor's cast.

Once 'twas busy planning, now 'tis trustful prayer;
Once 'twas anxious caring, now He has the care;
Once 'twas what I wanted, now what Jesus says;
Once 'twas constant asking, now 'tis ceaseless praise.

Once it was my working, His it hence shall be;
Once I tried to use Him, now He uses me;
Once the power I wanted, now the mighty One;
Once for self I labored, now for Him alone.[28]

THE ROAD TO DAMASCUS

The Apostle Paul, like everyone else, experienced the breaking process. Fortunately, he recorded for us not only the reasons, but also God's methods and the blessed results. Paul first tells us, "And because of the surpassing greatness of the revelations, for this reason, to keep me from exalting myself, there was given me a thorn in the flesh, a messenger of Satan to buffet me - to keep me from exalting myself!" (II Corinthians 12:7)

As to God's methods, Paul referred to them as "a thorn in the flesh" and "a messenger of Satan." Paul never tells us directly what the thorn/messenger was, but we can make some educated guesses, which most Biblical scholars agree upon. In any event, these assumptions do make some sense.

Paul was struck blind on the road to Damascus as part of his conversion experience. Although his eyesight was restored to some extent, it appears that Paul never fully recovered his eyesight. Paul told us he had received "visions and revelations," and ". . . heard inexpressible words, which a man is not permitted to speak." (II Corinthians 12:1 and 4) Having his eyesight permanently affected would be a constant and effective reminder to someone who had seen real visions and revelations.

In Paul's closing remarks in the Epistle to the Galatians, he says' "See with what large letters I am writing to you with my own hand." (Galatians 6:11) The Christians at Galatia were very aware and very sympathetic about Paul's vision problems. Paul wrote this about his

Galatian brethren, saying, "For I bear you witness, that if possible, you would have plucked out your eyes and given them to me." (Galatians 4: 15) This suggests that at least one thorn Paul had was very poor eyesight, probably since his encounter with Christ on the road to Damascus.

We also encounter what may have been another thorn or Satanic messenger in Paul's life. In Romans 7, Paul uses the Tenth Commandment, the sin of *coveting* to explain why the Law will never work in any person's life, including Paul's. His references to this sin indicates that coveting was a problem for him, and was even his undoing as a 'righteous' Pharisee. In any event, just like the rest of us, Paul wasn't perfect.

Acts 9 relates some of Paul's earlier adventures after his conversion. First, in Damascus he gained 'strength' as he argued that Jesus was the Christ. He caused so much trouble the Jews in Damascus were laying in wait to kill Paul. He escaped to Jerusalem, where he again stirred things up. Finally, the Apostles had had enough and sent Paul home to Tarsus in Asia Minor. The next verse, Acts 9:31 says, "So the church throughout all Judea and Galilee and Samaria enjoyed peace…" *Talk about a failed ministry.* Of course, God was not yet finished with Paul, and even though we struggle and fail, He is not finished with us either. But this **is** why brokenness is necessary!

Paul also learned an invaluable lesson through his difficulties, which he also shares with us. Concerning his thorn in the flesh, Paul prayed to the Lord three times that it might depart from him. It didn't. Does that mean Paul didn't have enough faith? Hardly, for it seems that the lesson Paul was taught was just the opposite, for Paul says the Lord said to him in response to his prayer, "My grace is sufficient for you, for power is perfected in weakness."

God's power is perfected in His follower's weaknesses. Paul's conclusion was, "Most gladly, therefore, I will rather boast about weaknesses, that the power of Christ may dwell in me. Therefore I am well content with weaknesses, with insults, with distresses, with persecutions, with difficulties, for Christ's sake; for when I am weak, then I am strong." (II Corinthians 12:8-10)

CONCLUSION

Over the years I have observed and counseled with many Christians who were struggling with their daily Christian lives. We all do at times. Sometimes it is a besetting sin we have to keep wrestling with; sometimes it is a failing family relationship; sometimes it is spiritual doubts and a lack of faith; and sometimes it is something a lot worse. By worse I mean the worst thing God has ever seen, probably beyond anything you have done and for sure beyond what you or I could even imagine.

My point is simply the only thing that can not be forgiven is dying without salvation. That immediately excludes all justified Christians. If you still question whether you have been justified, then it would be my bet that you are. Nevertheless, you are advised to reread this book and check out the Scriptures that are quoted or referred to.

I have just finished proofing this book for what seems like the zillionth time and even though I wrote it [with more help from God than I can even imagine], it still blesses me to review the sovereignty and greatness of our Lord and the inexhaustible riches and depth of His grace.

The Good News is the message of God' grace. It tells me that when I am weak then I am strong, and when I am feeling broken this is a blessing from God too. Also please keep in mind that there are *three more* volumes of *Making the Grace Connection: Living by Grace* to come soon!

May God truly bless you and I really mean it! Dave Ashwell

ENDNOTES

1 Encarta ® World English Dictionary © (P) 1998-2004 Microsoft Corporation.

2 William F. Beck, <u>The New Testament in the Language of Today</u> (5th ed.; St. Louis: Concordia Publishing House, 1964), p. xxvi

3 "Fire Insurance" refers to Evangelistic messages which reduce the gospel to nothing more than a way to avoid going to hell.

4 Encarta ® World English Dictionary © (P) 1998-2004 Microsoft Corporation.

5 Harold J. Grimm, <u>The Reformation Era 1500-1600</u> (2nd ed.; New York: The Macmillan Company, 1973), p. 121.

6 Correct Answers to the Reformation Quiz: 1-A, 2-A, 3-A, 4--B, 5-A, 6-B, 7-B, 8-A, 9-A, 10-B

7 The reference here is to the various positions Christians hold with regard to eschatology, the study of prophecies about the future. The three main schools of thought are the POST-MILLENIALLISTS, the A-MILLENIALLISTS, and the PRE-MILLENIALLISTS. Among the PRE-MILLENIALLISTS, there are an additional three groups, the PRE-TRIBULATIONISTS, the MID-TRIBULATIONISTS, and the POST-TRIBULATIONISTS. (A friend once suggested PAN-MILLENNIALISM as a solution, meaning it will all pan out in the end.)

8 Encarta ® World English Dictionary © (P) 1998-2004 Microsoft Corporation

9 R. C. Sproul, "The Pelagian Captivity of the Church," <u>Modern Reformation </u>, May/June 2001, Vol. 10, Number 3, p.22-29.

10 *Tetelestai* is the perfect, indicative, passive, third person singular of *teleo* meaning to finish or complete. *Tetelestai* thus means "it has been completed or finished" thus "Paid in Full." The papyri from the Alexandria, Egypt city dumps of the first century have yielded many such documents so marked.

Moulton, J. H. and Milligan, G., Vocabulary of the Greek New Testament, London, Hodder & Stoughton, 1930, p.630.

11 For those who are interested in a little more detail about the Greek language, the following is presented: As you know, the entire New Testament of the Bible is written in the Greek language. It is written in the *koine* or common everyday Greek everyone used, rather than the classical Greek of literature and drama. The particular genius of Greek is the precision of meaning it provides us. Greek verbs and participles have six different tenses, and four moods to further specify the writer's intent. The six tenses are the Future tense, the Present tense, and four Past tenses. The Future tense in Greek talks about things that either will happen or may happen depending on the mood of the verb. The Present tense describes activity that is currently on going, with out reference to a beginning or ending. The Imperfect tense, the first of our four past tenses, describes an ongoing activity in the past, without reaching attainment. The Aorist tense denotes activity or action that occurs at some point in time without any reference to its progress. The Perfect tense denotes a past action completed with its finished results evident in and affecting the present. The Pluperfect tense denotes a past action completed with its finished results also evident in the past, and no longer affecting the present.

Dana, H. E., and Mantey, Julius R., <u>A Manual Grammar of the Greek New Testament</u>, Toronto, The Macmillan Co., 1927 and 1955, pp. 176-208.

12 The charge against Jesus was that He made Himself out to be equal to or above the Roman Caesar. The penalty for this under Roman law was death by crucifixion. The charges were FALSE for two reasons. First, in His response to Pilate He pointed out that His kingdom was not of this world. The second reason, of course, was that He was indeed a greater ruler then any mere Roman Caesar! See John 18:33-19:22.

13 I Corinthians 1:18-31. A little true humility never hurt anyone.

14 This concept of losing one's salvation every time we sin was taught to me in a Bible college class by someone who should have known better. We must always be on your guard that what we are being taught is actually Biblical. Each of us is responsible to "test the spirits to see whether they are from God." I John 4:1

15 All humans are naturally disposed to WORKS of the LAW. This stems from our fallen estate in Adam, and the curses accompanying the knowledge of good and evil. In this fallen world, we 'work' for acceptance and 'earn' the respect of others by what we DO, not by who we are.

16 Encarta ® World English Dictionary © (P) 1998-2004 Microsoft Corporation.

17 The exception to this is the psychopathic personality [or sociopath]. These people tend to operate on the basis of immediate personal gratification without a moral or social conscience, which often leads to immoral and criminal behavior. Perhaps the loss of one's conscience is their compensation for being overwhelmed by guilt. [No conscience = no sin = no guilt]

18 At the time this letter was written, Paul was a prisoner in Rome, continuously shackled to various members of the Praetorian Guard. So he had every opportunity to closely study a Roman soldier's equipment.

19 Quoted from Wikipedia by Copyright © 2010 vBulletin Solutions, Inc. All rights reserved. SEO by vBSEO 3.5.1 ©2010, Crawlability, Inc.

20 Dan Edelen, The Battle for Brokenness (Cerulean Sanctum, Oct. 07, 2004).

21 John Newton, "Amazing Grace" in Hymns For The Family Of God, ed. by Fred Bock et. al., (Nashville: Paragon Associates, Inc., 1976), #107

22 From the Internet at http://www.cyberhymnal.org/bio/s/p/spafford_hg.htm

23 The disciple Peter saw John following them. He was the youngest of the Apostles, and the author of The Gospel According to John, I, II, and III John, and the book of Revelation. Read verses 23-24.

24 Retrieved from "http://en.wikipedia.org/wiki/History_of_salt"

25 Ibid.

26 We are also exhorted to be aware of Satan's desire to attack us, as we are told in I Peter 5:8. And we are warned to don the whole armor of God to protect us from the devil in Ephesians 6:10-20.

27 Every time Jesus uttered the phrase "truly, truly, I say to you, . . ." He was informing us that what He was about to say was and is of extreme importance!!

28 Dr. A. B. Simpson, <u>Himself</u>, quoted by V. Raymond Edman, <u>They Found The Secret</u> (Grand Rapids: Zondervan Publishing House, 1960) p. 8.